BE THE CHANGE

Other books by Zach Hunter:

*Generation Change: Roll Up Your Sleeves
and Change the World*

*Lose Your Cool: Discovering a Passion that
Changes You and the World*

UPDATED AND EXPANDED EDITION

BE THE CHANGE

YOUR GUIDE TO FREEING SLAVES AND CHANGING THE WORLD

ZACH HUNTER

ZONDERVAN®

ZONDERVAN.com/
AUTHORTRACKER
follow your favorite authors

We want to hear from you. Please send your comments about this book to us in care of zreview@zondervan.com. Thank you.

ZONDERVAN

Be the Change, Revised and Expanded Edition
Copyright © 2007, 2011 by Zach Hunter

This title is also available as a Zondervan ebook.
Visit www.zondervan.com/ebooks.

Requests for information should be addressed to:
Zondervan, Grand Rapids, Michigan 49530

Library of Congress Cataloging-in-Publication Data

Hunter, Zach.
    Be the change : your guide to freeing slaves and changing the world / Zach Hunter. — Updated and expanded ed.
    p. cm.
    ISBN 978-0-310-72611-1 (softcover)
    1. Teenagers—Religious life. 2. Love—Religious aspects—Christianity. 3. Liberty—Religious aspects—Christianity. 4. Antislavery movements—Moral and ethical aspects. 5. Dependency (Psychology). 6. Slavery—Moral and ethical aspects. I. Title.
BV4531.3.H86 2011
261.8'32—dc23   2011017986

Cover design: *Micah Kandros Design*
Cover photography: *Daley Hake*
Interior design and composition: *Greg Johnson/Textbook Perfect*

Printed in the United States of America

---

11 12 13 14 15 16 /DCI/ 22 21 20 19 18 17 16 15 14 13 12 11 10 9 8 7 6 5 4 3 2 1

Special Thanks

There are lots of people I want to thank for supporting me and believing God can use a kid to change the world. The people listed below are some of my favorite people in the world—and their encouragement has, in many ways, made it possible for me to write this book:

My parents; my little brother, Nate (another abolitionist); Steve Carter for allowing me to share my story; the Element gang, Uncle Ted Johnson, Ted Haddock; all the youth pastors I've ever had, each of whom has invested in my life (Nick Silvestro, Mike Rogalski, Kenny Schmitt); Christian David Turner; Jennifer Nix; Malcolm DuPlessis; Leeland; Jack and Shelly Mooring; Jeremiah Wood, Mike Smith; Jake Holtz; Darryl LeCompte; Brenton Brown; Brooke Fraser, my friends at CFS and PCA; Peter Furler; Troy and Sara Groves; Dan Haseltine and Charlie Lowell; Joel Houston and Hillsong United; Ty Anderson; Charlie Peacock; Jon Foreman; Roger Owens; Micheal Flaherty; Debbie Kovacs; Jennifer Lee; Clayton Ferguson; Erik Lokkesmoe and the whole Walden Media Experience and Walden Media staff; Sean Chapman; Justin McRoberts; Matt Maher; Bob Kilpatrick;

April Hefner; Given Kachepa; David Ngure; The Livingstone Collective; The Worship Together team; and Joseph Rojas.

I'm grateful to Ben Eisner; David Bean; Rich Mikan for saying yes to helping out a kid like me; the Parva, Broas, Rehfeld, Howell, and Robinson families who have my back in prayer; and Jamie Hinojosa for being a champion of this book.

Thanks to Jay Howver and the rest of the team at Youth Specialties and Zondervan, and to Doug Davidson for putting polish on my rough work. I also want to thank the leadership at Creation West, Spirit West Coast, Lifest, AtlantaFest, SoulFest, and Power of One for giving me opportunities to talk to my generation about God's heart for the oppressed. Thanks also to all of you whom I've met at festivals, speaking engagements, and on MySpace—you continue to encourage me as you lend your own voices to help bring freedom to victims of slavery.

> There is more hunger for love and appreciation in this world than for bread.

Mother Teresa (1910–1997)
Humanitarian, friend of the poor, and servant of God

DEDICATED
TO THOSE
WHO YEARN TO
BE FREE
AND THOSE
WHO SEEK TO
FREE THEM.

Table of Contents

Foreword

A Letter from Jon Foreman

Howdy friend!

I'm rooting for you, Zach.
Trust only the one who
empowers you to think and speak
and breathe differently than the
headlines. He who created the
foundations of the world is
still creating. His eyes
are on the oppressed and
the broken.

You've written a book. And yet, because words are so disposable in our culture your elders will say. "What can words do? Change never happens! What can be done!" Prove them wrong, Zach. Tell the story with your life.

About This Book

When I first started writing *Be the Change* I was fourteen years old. Since the book released, it's been a huge encouragement to hear from readers who are finding their own way to make a change in their communities and in the world. I'm now nineteen years old — still a teenager — but I've had the privilege of witnessing amazing things going on in my generation. In fact, as a result of everything that has happened in the past few years in the fight against slavery, I was asked to provide a few updates to this book so readers have the most-recent information and can continue to create change in the world around them.

Inside this new version of *Be the Change* you won't find heavily rewritten content — we decided to leave my fourteen-year-old voice and writing intact. But what you will find is some new content, updates on the fight against slavery, and some new information on a few of the personal stories in the book.

During the past five years I've traveled around much of the U.S. and other parts of the world learning more about the struggles many of our neighbors are facing and hearing how our generation is bringing relief. It's been an amazing, crazy adventure and I'm so happy to be able to continue to share it with you.

The fight for freedom is still on. And, while many people have responded to the call of being a voice for the voiceless, there is still much to be done, and much to be learned from the stories of the people that I wrote about in this book. Reading back through *Be The Change*, I'm struck by the lessons that I still have to learn from these stories that I thought I knew so well.

Progress

Since the release of *Be the Change* awareness has been heightened to the plight of those who've been exploited or enslaved. When I was twelve, not many people knew about the issue of modern-day slavery. To try to convince people, especially adults, that slavery existed (even on U.S. soil) was quite a feat. But even before it became a hot-button cultural issue, a fashionable phenomenon, there were young people getting involved simply because it's the right thing to do. In the past five years there have been several award-winning films, documentaries, books, and conferences about the issue of modern-day slavery. I still run into people occasionally who are completely unaware of the slave trade, but it's much less common to talk to someone who has no idea people are being bought and sold.

It's been said that the first step in ending an atrocity is having people aware of the fact that it's occurring. On that front, we're making some progress. But with millions of people still enslaved, and corruption and exploitation thriving in many corners of the world, we still have much to do.

What I think is really cool is that students have been using what they have at their disposal, the skills or assets that they've been given, to fight against slavery. I just want to cover three areas of society where a lot has happened in the area of social justice and the abolitionist movement in the past few years.

The Church

I love seeing followers of Jesus living out their faith and looking for ways to demonstrate to a suffering world that God is good. You'd be hard-pressed to find a church that hasn't incorporated some form of social justice (though they may not call it that) into their mission and outreach. There are entire churches that have become abolitionist churches, and, more specifically, more youth groups across the world have started Loose Change to Loosen Chains programs. Many youth groups are taking a serious look at what it means to love God by loving their neighbor.

Churches are treating those who are being exploited and those in extreme poverty as if those individuals were Jesus. We are realizing that people of faith are required to help those in need. It is an integral part of our lives—something not to be left just for clergy or career missionaries. This is really encouraging to me, but I also have a caution. I'm concerned that this not become a fad or a trend in church growth strategies. Instead, I'm hoping we see this become a part of our DNA as global Christians—something that's ingrained into us and is an outworking of our faith. I also hope we can see the necessary balance of studying and knowing the Bible so we will know how to live in a suffering world while reaching out and offering the hope Jesus has given us. No pendulum swings and extremes, but a faith accompanied by works and a compassionate life of grace. Our freedom was bought at a high price and we need to use our freedom to help free others.

Governments

Several years ago, the U.S. government started the Trafficking in Persons (TIP) office to monitor and snuff out human trafficking. Governments laced with corruption and who look the other way when people are being sold are being exposed. For the first time the TIP office is now ranking the United States in these areas — exposing where trafficking is occurring and what's being done to fight it.

In the U.S., local law enforcement said that it was difficult to find and address situations of trafficking ... and girls who were forced to be prostitutes were treated as criminals because law enforcement didn't know what to do with them. In the past five years we've seen community groups, churches, and nonprofits come together and work with police to identify cases of trafficking, arrest the perpetrators, and help restore the dignity of the victims. Churches are becoming resources for local government officials and helping treat victims as victims by providing safe aftercare and a place to rebuild their lives.

There are more cases being tried and more perpetrators being held accountable around the world. People are getting educated about how to spot a victim of trafficking and how to report an abuse. These are all good signs.

Corporations

A lot of you may have heard of or purchased Fair Trade goods. More and more products are readily available that we can be sure are slave-free: chocolate, coffee, textiles, furniture, rugs. Now there are also a lot of "better than fair trade" products — where corporations are investing back into the community, supporting local farmers and workers, and helping rescue people from poverty.

Reforms are being made — even in industries that have historically been terrible in the area of human rights. For instance, in the chocolate industry even the big corporations are coming to the table to discuss how to clean up their practices. We're not there yet, but I hope to see a day when all of the big chocolate companies are slave-free. But for now, it's really easy to walk into a Whole Foods or Costco and buy chocolate that is slave-free.

It's not abnormal to see popular products with a cause integrated into their business model. There are also companies like TOMS Shoes and Project 7 who have built into their product a charitable giving component, triggered each time you buy something from them. It is becoming increasingly possible to fight slavery, recognize companies that are doing good, and not using slave labor. To stay up to date on advancements being made, visit *www.zachhunter.me* and click on "Loose Change to Loosen Chains."

Thanks so much for taking the time to read a book written by a fourteen-now-nineteen-year-old, and for believing in our generation. Rhetoric aside, I do believe we can change the world—perhaps in small ways on a daily basis, and I and other social reformers want you to be a part of it. My hope is this book might play a role as a catalyst for your efforts to bring hope and help.

You'll find that each chapter is organized around a theme or key word, and concludes with some questions for reflection and discussion. You may want to read this book alone and use these questions as a launching pad for journaling or a time of silence with God. Or you might want to get together with a few friends or discipleship group and explore the questions together.

There are also lots of suggestions for how to put into action what you're learning. Sometimes these are very personal points of action, and other times they are things you'd do with other people. The goal is for us all to work together to bring about an amazing change—first in ourselves, and then in the world.

I believe God calls us to live in ways that will make a difference and be an inspiration. Get inspired yourself. I hope this book will be a tool to help us on this journey together, realizing that God can use us all to be the change!

INSPIRATION

"iF YOU WANT TO
LiFT YOURSELF UP,
LiFT UP SOMEONE ELSE."

Booker T. Washington (1856–1915)
Emancipated slave, intellectual, and education reformer

Dreaming Big

Everyone wants their life to leave a print in the wet concrete of history. When little boys and girls are asked, "What do you want to be when you grow up?," no one says "a loser." When kids are asked what they want to do with their lives, they never say, "I hope I'll live a few years and no one remembers me." Most kids dream of being superheroes, fighting villains, winning battles.

Well, I still have those big dreams. And I believe God likes it when his kids dream big. I'd just turned fourteen years old when I started writing this book, and I'm a modern-day abolitionist. Some of you might be hearing that word for the first time and going, "What in the world is an abolitionist?" An abolitionist is someone who's committed to ending slavery. When I was twelve I started a campaign called Loose Change to Loosen Chains to motivate students to get involved in freeing slaves.

Maybe you think slavery was eliminated a long time ago. That's what a lot of people think. Unfortunately, it's not true. That's right, slavery still goes on *today*.

I first heard about the plight of modern-day slaves around age twelve. I had been studying the history of slavery in the United States and learned about Harriet Tubman, a former slave who went on to help free many other slaves. I remember telling my mom, "Man, if I had lived back then, I would have fought for equality, and against slavery." But then my mom told me slavery was still going on throughout the world in many ways, shapes, and forms. My mom was working for an organization that frees modern-day slaves around the world, and she was learning about many forms of slavery for the first time. I, too, realized slavery is not just some outdated thing you read about in your history books. When I found out slavery still occurs today, I was furious. But I knew it wasn't enough to simply feel bad about the issue. Emotions are only useful when they motivate us into action. I had to do something.

Modern slavery takes many ugly forms. It can be anything from whole families getting into medical debt and having to work in a brickyard till they die; to little girls working in brothels; to kids being forced to roll cigarettes all day long. *In fact, there are actually more slaves in the world today than there were during the entire transatlantic slave trade!*

You may be wondering how people become slaves. Many think it all starts with a dramatic kidnapping, but that is rarely the case. Usually it has to do with money, or lack of it. Sometimes a family allows a child to go with a trusted family friend who promises a good job to help meet the family's needs. The child soon discovers this "friend" has sold them into slavery. Or, in some instances, a desperate parent will actually sell their own child into slavery. Often the parents are misled to believe their child will have better living conditions and maybe an opportunity for a better education. Instead, the child becomes a slave.

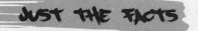

JUST THE FACTS

27 Million: Number of people in modern-day slavery around the world

Sources: Free the Slaves — cited by **The New York Times,** *United Nations, and many others*

One recent story of a modern-day slave girl involves a child whose mother had died and whose father remarried. Not only did her new mother not like her, but her father had a drinking problem. He sold his young daughter into slavery to get her out from under his new wife's feet and to help fund his addiction to alcohol. Like many other children, this elementary-aged girl was forced to spend her days rolling little cigarettes called "Beedies." These kids have to sit on the floor, rolling the cigarettes with their tiny fingers and poking the ends in with a sharp knife. Their fingers are cut and cracked from the work. Many times they are beaten if they don't reach their work quota. (By the way, some American teens think it's cool to smoke these cigarettes, but in doing so they are fueling the slave trade.)

When I hear about situations like these, I feel motivated to do something. So for the last few years I've been doing what I can to end these oppressive practices. In the summer of 2006 I went on a speaking tour where I've had the chance to talk to hundreds of thousands of people about this issue. Some of my speaking has been connected with a film called *Amazing Grace*

that deals with the historic slave trade and how we can continue
the work of abolition. It tells the story of William Wilberforce,
a young British politician and abolitionist. Like Wilberforce, I've
had the chance to talk with politicians, but with my efforts I've
mainly been targeting other teens and twenty-somethings. But
it's a message for everyone. I'm convinced it will take people
from all walks of life, of all age groups and economic back-
grounds, to end the sale of humans.

People Who Inspire Me

People sometimes ask who or what inspires me. I usually answer
by talking about some of the historic people I write about in this
book, such as William Wilberforce and Mother Teresa. I've discovered there's a lot you can learn from these dead people—and we
have the luxury of looking back and seeing the impact they made.

Some of the people who inspire me most today are people
in my life you've probably never heard of. (I've mentioned some
of them on my thanks page—check them out!) I'm sure that's true
for you too. All of us know people in our lives who have made
a profound impact on who we are and how we live. One of the
people who most inspires me is my dad. When I was eleven he
was diagnosed with a brain tumor. We didn't know how serious it
was for a while; later my mom and dad were told he would probably die. Throughout that time my dad was completely at peace.
We went to several neurosurgeons, and they recommended we

"There is a yearning for justice inherent in the lining of every heart, and a sense encircling every synapse that tells us things are not as they ought to be in this world. But it is a glorious and unique endeavor to fight against the disconnect of our privileged culture and start to breathe and move and embody the mandate to act on the yearnings, and respond to the senses, and ultimately live as if the Gospel is true, and freedom and justice are worth every ounce of blood, muscle, and thought we could possibly offer."

Dan Haseltine
Jars of Clay/Blood: Water Mission

go to Duke University Medical Center. He got an MRI there, and they found out the tumor hadn't been growing, that it was basically dead tissue. This was fantastic news — but I think my dad's attitude would have been the same even if the news had been terrible. He had trusted God from the beginning. My dad is one of my favorite people, and one of the strongest people I know.

My mom also inspires me. She plays many roles, not only of "soccer mom," but also runs a business and works for several clients at a time. My mom stands with me in my work as an abolitionist. I probably will never know all she's done for me, but I'm grateful for her. I love her a lot. She is also one of my favorite people, and is extremely talented and caring.

I'm also inspired by the many other people working for justice today, such as a former slave named Given Kachepa, whom I met not long ago. You'll hear more about him in this book too. You'll read a lot about the issue of slavery — because it's my personal passion. But you'll also read about other people and stories that inspire me. And, I hope, you'll likewise be inspired to change this world.

Before we dive into those stories, I want to say a little bit about my generation. What I love is how expressive we are, and how much we care about the world when we are confronted with issues of suffering and oppression. I am inspired by the many other students I meet who want to show their love of God by loving people. Of course, I've heard people — adults —

"Tell a man he is brave, and you help him become so."

Thomas Carlyle (1795–1881)
Scottish historian and essayist

complaining about how my generation is selfish, and how little we listen, and how we are rebellious. But those problems aren't unique to our generation—I think we've had a lot of "good" examples to show us how to be this way. I think we need people to come along and be a better example. That is part of what I am trying to do through this book and through my campaign. Our generation needs somebody to set the bar high for us so we will have something to live up to, and even live beyond.

I'm excited about my generation. I think God just might use us to change the world—we have the passion and the energy. I want to encourage us to spend (or maybe better put, invest) our youth for Jesus. I'm up for it; are you? I believe by working side by side with God doing the things he loves—like seeking justice, loving mercy, helping those in need—we learn more about God and more about ourselves. I don't believe we have

to do things for God to get closer to him and win his approval.
But I do believe that if we love God, we will want to serve him
and others. I also think it's pretty cool God wants us to join him
in this effort when he really doesn't need our help to do anything! He's more than capable.

INFLUENCE

"SPEAK UP FOR THOSE
WHO CANNOT SPEAK FOR THEMSELVES,
FOR THE RIGHTS OF ALL
WHO ARE DESTITUTE.
SPEAK UP AND JUDGE FAIRLY;
DEFEND THE RIGHTS OF THE
POOR AND NEEDY."

Proverbs 31:8 - 9

Take a Look at Influence

Josiah Wedgwood

Josiah Wedgwood was a British tycoon. He traded in stocks, owned a profitable business, and developed one of the most successful fashion trends ever. In fact, his label was all over clothes and jewelry. By the way, he lived two hundred years ago.

Josiah Wedgwood started out as a simple potter, earning his living as a thrower (someone who makes pottery with a potter's wheel). But before he could really master his craft he got a terrible case of smallpox, which led to the amputation of one of his legs. Throwing was a physically demanding job in which you had to pump the pedal that turned the disk the clay sat on. After losing one of his legs, Wedgwood could no longer throw pottery. But Josiah Wedgwood wasn't one to give up.

Instead, he focused on designing pottery and jewelry, and practiced a form of pottery that did not involve a potter's wheel. He experimented with glazes and formulas until he developed a beautiful cream-colored pottery that was extremely popular, mainly because Queen Charlotte loved it. That was probably why the pottery was dubbed "Queen's Ware." I guess things weren't much different from the way they are today—if someone really famous loves a product, then others will buy it. Eventually, Wedgwood became very rich and influential.

One of Wedgwood's friends was Thomas Clarkson, a notable abolitionist of his time. (Clarkson was a member of the Clapham

Sect. I'll say more about that group in the next chapter.) Clarkson encouraged Wedgwood to use his influence by taking a stand on the controversial issue of the slave trade, and Wedgwood did. Josiah Wedgwood came out with a popular jewelry piece called the slave medallion. It had an African slave in shackles saying, "Am I not a man and a brother?"

This piece spread like wildfire. In no time, people were buying all sorts of jewelry and other items—snuff boxes, brooches, hat pins—all with the slave medallion on them. It was the label everyone was wearing—kind of like today's "Live Strong" bracelet or the red AIDS ribbon, except the slave medallion was bigger. *Much* bigger. It became so popular and had so many uses that Thomas Clarkson noted, "Ladies wore them in bracelets, and others fitted them up in an ornamental manner as pins for their hair. At length the taste for wearing them became general, and thus fashion, which usually confines itself to worthless things, was seen once in the honorable office of promoting the cause of justice, humanity, and freedom."

Wedgwood continued in his support of the anti-slavery movement, even though this could have cost him his business and popularity. But he was committed to the cause of abolition and spoke up anyway. Ironically, he actually ended up richer than before.

Josiah Wedgwood died before he could witness the abolition of the slave trade in his homeland. But he set the standard for using a brand to do good.

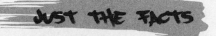

17,500: Number of foreign nationals who are trafficked into the U.S. every year

Sources: U.S. House of Representatives and the Polaris Project, among others

Another Look at Influence

Artists and Their Brands

Who's really influential today? What names come to mind when you think of influential or famous people? Most people tend to think of movie stars, recording artists, or athletes. If you've noticed, those are the people who are usually sought after for their endorsements. That's why you see the face of LeBron James on bubble gum, Carrie Underwood wearing Skechers, and Johnny Depp's image on candy and toys. It's all about influence — and money. Endorsements are big business, and the bigger the name, the more money a star can get for selling products. Many stars have now begun to use their influence not only to pedal product, but to raise awareness and funds to help others who can't help themselves. In fact, it's become expected. Just about every actor, designer, or musician I can think of is speaking out for a cause.

Take Jon Foreman, frontman for the Grammy-Award-winning band Switchfoot. He had it made — a double-platinum-selling album, his songs appearing in feature films, playing concerts to sold-out crowds around the world. But that wasn't enough for him.

On a trip to India, Jon learned of the plight of the Dalit people. Let me take a minute to explain who the Dalits are. India's society features a caste system, which is a set of rigid rules that divide people into groups based on their social class. Within this system the Dalits are viewed as the lowest of the low. They are not given access to the rights and benefits other people enjoy in their country. They are viewed as "untouchable" and less than equal and are oppressed in terrible ways. While those born into India's upper castes retain most of the society's wealth, those in the lowest castes often find it impossible to better their situation, no matter what they do. Because of this, many Dalits are enslaved in their own country and spend their lives working against their will in rock quarries, brick kilns, or match factories, or making other products.

CHECK OUT

www.switchfoot.com

www.facelessinternational.com

www.bloodwatermission.com

www.jarsofclay.com

www.anberlin.com

www.saragroves.com

www.thehomefoundation.net

INFLUENCE

When I met Jon Foreman in Atlanta, we talked about modern-day slavery and why he takes time to educate others about what he's learned about the Dalit people. He feels there has to be a way to use art and music to bring the story of the people he's met to the mainstream. Like many artists, Jon thinks creatively and believes God has a purpose in fame. Jon and his Switchfoot bandmates use their platform to raise awareness not only about the Dalits but also about others who suffer injustice in the world. They've raised money for Habitat for Humanity, worked to bring relief to Haiti, partnered on local programs to feed the homeless, and have helped children in Africa get an education. Jon's using his influence to speak out for people who don't have a voice, bringing their plight to the attention of millions of people around the world who might be able to help.

Another guy who's using his influence for good is Stephen Christian from the band Anberlin. Not only is Stephen a cool guy, he also has a childlike care for the hurting. You know what I mean? Remember when you were really little and you saw someone else get hurt? You wanted to help them immediately—no excuses about why it didn't make sense or why it wasn't practical. It bothered you to see someone cry or be mistreated, and you were willing to share a toy or give something of your own to help someone who was sad or hurting.

Well, Stephen still has this same instinct to care. He could shut himself up in his tour bus and hide from the world, but instead he has chosen to open his head and heart to the hurting in the world. Stephen has taken a group of musicians to Haiti and has made several similar trips to India. His goal with these trips is not only to expose other people to the realities facing the poor in such countries, but also to look for ways to help. Stephen started an organization called Faceless to help address some of the needs he's encountering. He isn't interested in taking another missions trip that makes him feel good about himself. He wants to change the world.

Why would Dan Haseltine from Jars of Clay found an organization called Blood:Water Mission to bring clean water to Africa? Why do artists like Sara Groves and Natalie Grant travel to the far corners of the world to witness suffering firsthand? It's because they believe in a big God who has big ideas to bring big relief to the oppressed. Like U2's Bono, who once said he wanted to invest his fame in "things that matter," these people know their influence counts for something. And while fame may be fleeting, it is worth a lot in the moment.

What about You?

Living Out Influence Today

Another way to look at influence is to consider what marketers call "branding." You're familiar with the brands you buy and can recognize them easily by their logos. When you see the "swoosh" you think Nike, just as when you see the little white apple you think Mac or iPod/iPad. Millions of dollars are spent to get you to remember these brands and their slogans. And, as I've mentioned, connecting celebrity to brands makes them even more powerful and memorable.

But have you ever considered *your* brand? Well, each one of us has his or her own brand — even if we're still in school. Whether you're Nerd, Jock, or Hipster (or, to be more politically correct, Academic, Athlete, or Artist), everyone has a brand. Your brand is who people know you to be. It's your reputation.

Now these brands aren't always a good thing. They can lead to prejudice or a cliquish environment in which we hang out only with people who have the same brand as us. This is wrong. Instead of using our brands to exclude others, why don't we use them to help others? Whatever our brands give us access to, let's utilize it. Just because we're young doesn't mean our voices don't matter and our brands don't carry power and influence. The Bible says "even small children are known by their actions" (Proverbs 20:11). This means we can't be let off the hook just because we are young. We can't just sit back and expect our elders to do all the work.

I'm hopeful because I really believe our generation has the power and passion to change things. I know some really great guys in a band called Leeland — they're from a small town in Texas. The band started out leading worship in their church, but they've come a long way since then. They've traveled the world and played at some of the largest music festivals in the country. These young guys are way more mature than many people older than them. They are some of the most talented, godliest guys I know.

The summer I met them I was fourteen years old and I was speaking at a music festival, leading seminars on justice and abolition. The lead singer of the band, Leeland Mooring, was listening—I think he was seventeen or eighteen at the time. He and the others in the band (which now includes Leeland's siblings Jack and Shelly, and their friend Mike Smith) had never heard about modern-day slavery. It blew them away that something as heinous as slavery is still going on today, especially when they found out many of the slaves are children and teens like us! That day I told the story of a teenager who worked as a slave in a rock quarry and ended up having her finger amputated. (She and her family were later rescued, along with many other slaves, through the efforts of an organization I support through Loose Change to Loosen Chains.) I also talked about some of the many passages like Isaiah 1:17 that speak of how God calls us to seek justice and rescue the oppressed.

The guys from Leeland began exploring further what God says about justice in Scripture and got involved. They didn't second-guess their convictions; they stepped up and began using their influence to help kids held in slavery, speaking from the stage to urge people to get involved. They are also involved with Food for the Hungry, further using their brand to help others.

I think that's what our generation should be about. We can pick up where other generations left off. Lots of people have tried to label our generation. Well, I'd like to see us known as the "Justice Generation" or JGEN. If we can harness the power of our individual brands, strengths, and passions, and use them for good, just imagine what we could get done working together with God. Let's get busy!

"God has a plan to help bring justice to the world — and his plan is us."

Gary Haugen
President of International Justice Mission

The Amazing Change

Influence in Action

What kind of benefit can people like Stephen Christian, Jon Foreman, and other artists bring to causes? How important could this be?

Read Luke 4:14–20. Whom did Jesus come to speak up for? How should this impact how you use your "brand" or influence?

How do others view our generation? How do you want our generation to be viewed?

Who influences you? Whom do you influence?

How can students use their own "brand" for good?

Ponder Proverbs 31:8-9 and consider how it relates to using your "brand" and influence.

Influence

Be the Change!

On the back of the title page for this chapter, write down how you would describe your brand. What would your slogan be? What do you want to be known for?

List two ways that you can use your own influence to help some-one else.

Pray for celebrities who can use their influence to reach and help millions of people. Pray they will have generous hearts and will take advantage of opportunities they have to do good.

CHECK OUT

www.zachhunter.me for news about what celebrities and influencers are doing to bring hope and help to the world.

COMMUNITY

"NEVER DOUBT THAT A SMALL GROUP
OF THOUGHTFUL, COMMITTED CITIZENS
CAN CHANGE THE WORLD,
INDEED IT'S THE ONLY THING THAT EVER HAS."

Margaret Mead (1901–1978)
Anthropologist and author

Take a Look at Community

Clapham

In the nineteenth century, the little village of Clapham in England was home to a group of friends who tackled the tough issues of their day. Their opponents called them the "Clapham Sect" — and the name stuck. Many of these friends were ministers or politicians, and one was a playwright. Each person had different strengths and skills, which made for a pretty powerful community.

Clapham was beautiful and peaceful — the kind of place you might go to get away from the craziness of life. But things weren't always tranquil in Clapham. As a matter of fact, when certain issues came up, things could get very tense! Members of the sect often discussed the key political ideas of the day. When they disagreed with one another, they debated. But when they agreed, they went out and fought for change together.

One issue they agreed on was the abolition of the slave trade. Members of the sect often met together in the home of William Wilberforce or Henry Thornton — two of their leaders — to discuss the issue. As a young man, Wilberforce decided his faith would impact what he did with his life. Fighting slavery became one of his main goals.

These friends also shared something else in common: They were all evangelical Christians. Their faith was what motivated them to change things. They weren't satisfied when they knew

45

others were suffering if they thought they had the power to help. They accomplished many things together: sending out missionaries, establishing what we now call Sunday schools, starting the Royal Society for the Prevention of Cruelty to Animals, and other efforts to improve society. But they are most known for the abolition of the slave trade.

As part of their abolition efforts, they worked to develop and support a colony of freed slaves living in Sierra Leone, Africa. The people of Clapham didn't just involve themselves in problems in their immediate neighborhood; they were willing to help people they'd never met, or people who were very different from them. They were like one family, combining their diverse strengths and unified passion to go after what seemed like impossible projects—attacking difficult ills of society with the tenacity of a fleet of battleships.

That's often how things get done—a group of friends with different talents and a common goal, working together to accomplish something none of them could do alone.

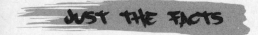

JUST THE FACTS

50: The number of U.S. states with reported cases of human trafficking

Source: U.S. Department of Education

Another Look at Community

Mike, Trey, Jedd, and Matt

I recently read a great book called *Four Souls*. It was written by four guys who go in search of what they call "the epic life." They were all in their early twenties, heading toward their careers, but these friends decided to take a detour and explore the world. The guys were drastically different from one another. For example, one was an optimist; another, a born leader. The differences that made their friendships interesting also caused them to get on one another's nerves from time to time. So while they were deliberately trying to grow together in their faith and develop real and honest friendships, there were times when their frustration with one another brought out the worst in them.

Everywhere they went, they looked for places to serve. Whether they were in Bangladesh or rural Vietnam, they took advantage of opportunities to help others and demonstrate what it means to be a follower of Jesus. They showed the *Jesus* film to former KGB agents, built churches, played soccer with kids, cleaned up communities, and were on the ultimate missions adventure for about seven months. They covered for one another in times of need—when one of them was having a rough day, another would fill in and do whatever needed to be done. If one guy was sick from a parasite, or just lonely, another "brother" was there to pick him up.

There's no way so much would have been accomplished if any of them had made this journey alone. That's what community is about—looking out for one another and keeping one another safe and accountable. Community isn't without its tough days—but they learned you can come through the rough spots and be stronger if you stick together and don't give up.

"Two are better than one, because they have a good return for their work: If one falls down, his friend can help him up. But pity the man who falls and has no one to help him up!"

Ecclesiastes 4:9-10

What about You?

Living Out Community Today

It's hard for teens to be in true community. We are all so different from one another, and we normally gravitate toward people who are like us. Being a teen is hard. It's hard to find your niche—and once you do, you want to protect it. So it's easy to get territorial and feel afraid to let in anyone new. Sometimes you may feel you don't really want to explore outside your pod of friends because it threatens your identity. So you end up living in a very small world of people just like you. Face it—that sounds pretty boring!

If you eavesdrop on conversations in a high school cafeteria, you don't hear much that's really interesting. There aren't a lot of sincere conversations about things that really matter. Most of the talk is about the things people have in common and what somebody did over the weekend. But true community is more than this. I think community happens when a group of people meet together and can be honest with one another about what really matters. It's a place where you can be accountable, where you can explore new ideas together, and where everyone is accepted. It's a safe place where you trust people and know they have your back.

I have been looking for this kind of community—and although I haven't really found it yet, I'm hopeful. I get together with a group of guys from my church each week. We're all really different, and I think we could all be good friends. I think we could challenge one another and keep one another accountable. But that takes a lot of work. And time, which is something teens aren't known for wanting to invest.

Jesus and his twelve disciples are a great model of community. They were very different—a carpenter, a political activist, a few fishermen, and a doctor. There were rich and poor. There were hard-working laborers as well as a guy who earned his living by taking other people's money—a tax collector. Man, these guys were different! They didn't all belong to the same country club and probably didn't even listen to the same kind of music. There was one guy who said everything that was on his mind (Peter), and one who rarely said what he thought (James). All those differences seem like the perfect setting for the perfect storm—or at least a daily, annoying drizzle.

It's strange, isn't it, that this was Jesus' model for how he would do ministry? But if it worked for him, maybe we should give it a try. It's messy, getting close to other people. It means humbling yourself and sticking your neck out. You'll probably get hurt, and you'll probably hurt others. But it seems like a risk worth taking—'cause the payoff could be really big.

The Amazing Change

Community in Action

Is your circle of friends filled mostly with people a lot like you? Why?

Think about someone you've met recently who is very different from you. Why might that person be interesting to get to know? What could you learn from that person?

Do you seek out conversations about important issues that impact you or the world, or do you avoid such discussions? How about discussing your faith and how things are going between you and God?

Have your friendships progressed through seasons like those of the guys from *Four Souls* — where things that didn't used to bug you about someone now do? What do you think about the idea that working through those times can actually make your friendships stronger?

Have you ever tackled something with a community of people? How was the task made easier by working together? Were there ways that working together made it harder? How?

Is it possible to have different groups of friends for different purposes in your life? Explain what that looks like.

Community

Be the Change!

On the back of the title page for this chapter, write three things you'd like to accomplish in a community of friends. (For example, you might want to launch a missions project, or grow in your relationship with Christ, or tackle something new.)

Pray that God would help you gather the right people to work with you. Remember, these may not be people in your existing circle of friends, and they may not be like you. Ask God to keep you open to working with new people and learning from them.

List a couple of people on the "Community" page you've met in the past year with whom you've not pursued a friendship, but whom you think God could use in your life. Make a point to cook them out this week.

COURAGE

"HISTORY, DESPITE ITS WRENCHING PAIN,
CANNOT BE UNLIVED,
BUT IF FACED WITH COURAGE,
NEED NOT BE LIVED AGAIN."

Maya Angelou (born 1928)
Poet, author, and civil-rights activist

Take a Look at Courage

Harriet Tubman

The woman the world knows as Harriet Tubman was born Araminta Ross, the fourth of nine children of two slaves, Ben and Harriet Greene Ross. At the tender age of seven, this little slave girl was torn away from her family and sent to work for another master. Imagine being in her shoes. Plantation slave quarters were all Araminta had ever known, and while it was not the life she would have chosen, it was familiar. Imagine the courage it must have taken for her to not despair when it seemed she would never see her family again.

She was taken to a little cabin owned by the Cook family. They made a small living because Mr. Cook was a trapper and Mrs. Cook was a weaver. Araminta (or Minty, as she was called) worked as their slave doing work around the house. Mrs. Cook tried to get Minty to wind yarn for her, but Minty kept sneezing, and she was too slow. So Mrs. Cook sent Minty outside to Mr. Cook because she was fed up with her. Mr. Cook taught her how to watch his traps and haul them in when muskrats crawled into them. These are not the kind of chores you'd expect from a young child. I can't imagine what it must have been like for this little girl; no mom to comfort her, no dad to care for her.

One day Minty got the measles. She was forced to continue working even though many children died from the measles during that time. When she finally collapsed, the Cooks took her back to her old plantation to be nursed back to health by her parents. She recovered quickly, but her voice remained raspy and husky for her entire life because of the bronchitis that came with the measles. When she was well she was sent back to the Cooks, who almost immediately sent her back to the plantation, saying she was stupid and clumsy. She was very happy to be back with her family, but she still had to work. And when the slave master had a bad season and his crops didn't bring in enough money, he sold Minty again to another family. She represented cash to him. So this little girl once again had to leave her family. Remember how scared you felt going to kindergarten for the first time, or being dropped off somewhere by your parents when you were little? Well, imagine how much worse it had to be for Minty. Imagine the courage she had to muster up just to make it through each day.

The new family had a baby, and Minty's job was to take care of the baby. She was expected to sleep right next to the cradle and rock it whenever the baby cried (which was often). Minty also was supposed to keep house and help around the kitchen. The slave mistress was often in a bad mood, and didn't like Minty anyway, so she often whipped her. One day Minty saw her mistress coming at her with the whip, so she ran out to the pig pen and stayed there for almost a week, fighting the pigs for their food. She made it back to her old plantation, where her mother worked to help her heal from the deep whip marks left by her old mistress. When she was well enough, she was forced to work as a field hand. She was only ten years old! What were you doing when you were ten? Can you imagine what this girl had gone through?

Minty continued working in the fields for several more years. By age thirteen she was almost as strong as a grown man! Then one day, when Minty was in town at the dry goods store picking something up for her "owners," she saw a slave from a nearby farm with his overseer running after him. The slave had gone to town without permission, and the overseer was furious. He demanded that Minty apprehend the slave so he could take him back to the farm and punish him. When Minty refused the overseer threw a heavy metal brick (which was used to balance the scales in the store) at the runaway, but hit Minty instead! She took a brick in the head for another slave.

News of Minty's bold refusal to help capture the escaped slave spread until she was given her adult name: Harriet. Once again she was nursed back to health by her mother. But her head injury had some lingering effects. Sometimes she would just fall into a deep sleep, much like a coma. As a result no one wanted to buy Harriet, and when the next chain gang came to her plantation, she and two of her brothers were sold into it.

After leaving the plantation, Harriet married a free black man named John Tubman. Yet she yearned for her own freedom and began to plan an escape. She told John of her plan, but he said he no longer loved her and would tell her master if she tried to run away. But she was committed to be free. And finally, one day, Harriet and three of her brothers escaped and headed for the North.

After all she'd been through, you might think Harriet would have stayed in the safety of the North. But she knew there were many people still enslaved in the South who needed to be rescued. So Harriet Tubman returned to the South many times, orchestrating the journey to freedom for hundreds of other slaves. She had learned courage as a young girl, and that courage served her and others well as she faced terrible risks to help emancipate other slaves. There was a bounty on her head, and she knew getting caught would mean her death.

It's estimated that Harriet Tubman helped three hundred people escape from slavery. I could go on and on with different tales of the people Harriet led to freedom through the Underground Railroad. If you haven't read her whole story, you should check it out. You'll see what true courage is all about.

Another Look at Courage

How I Found It

In May 2006, I was given an opportunity to speak about the issue of modern-day slavery at a big music festival in California. There were nearly 15,000 people there — one of the biggest crowds I'd ever seen, let alone spoken to!

"When a resolute young fellow steps up to the great bully, the world, and takes him boldly by the beard, he is often surprised to find it comes off in his hand, and that it was only tied on to scare away the timid adventurers."

Ralph Waldo Emerson (1803–1882)
Author, poet, philosopher

Most people don't know I struggled with an anxiety disorder when I was in elementary school. I would experience short periods of depression, felt paranoid, and was scared of getting sick. It was mainly because I was scared of throwing up. See, I'd once had this really bad virus—like the stomach flu except much worse. I was sick for a long time and I think my memory of the illness kind of haunted me even after I was well. During these anxiety attacks, I would either have trouble breathing or I'd get extremely nauseated. Sometimes, I'd just lie down and it felt as though I couldn't get up. These attacks were making me miserable most of the time, and robbing me of my joy and courage.

Through support from family, God, and friends, I defeated my anxiety disorder, and I haven't had an attack in several years. But when I looked out at that huge crowd at that music festival, some of those old fears came rushing back.

I remember looking out on the stage where David Crowder was just getting ready to perform and thinking there was no way I could do this. And I remember turning to my mom and saying, "I don't think I can go up there."

Mom responded, "That's okay, then don't." I don't know if she was serious or not. But I knew I had the chance to let people know the story of the millions of people who are suffering around the world as slaves. And if I didn't speak up, then who would?

With the promise of my mom praying for me, I decided to go ahead and take the stage, trusting God would give me the courage when I got there. I explained the truth of slavery to thousands of people that night, and I'm glad I did. That summer I was able to speak to nearly half a million people about slavery, God's passion for justice, and how they can get involved in helping to end slavery forever. God has given me a spirit of peace as I speak up for others. I know I have courage that comes from him, and that he is the one who enables me to do what I do. I occasionally get nervous, but the stories of kids who are in slavery compel me to be courageous.

I know the courage I need to show is really nothing compared to the courage of many others who face death and danger every day. Soldiers who put their lives on the line to defend their countries. Investigators who brave dark corners of the world to free slaves. Firefighters who enter burning buildings to risk their lives for one more victim. And certainly, the courage required of me doesn't compare to the courage required of every man, woman, and child in slavery who must wake up today and face their oppressors. But each of us faces situations in which we need to gather up our courage. When we do, it's as though the courage multiplies like yeast in dough, allowing us to be even more courageous the next time we're called upon.

"You gain strength, courage, and confidence by every experience in which you really stop to look fear in the face. You must do the thing which you think you cannot."

Eleanor Roosevelt (1884–1962)
U.S. political leader and human rights activist

What about You?

Living Out Courage Today

Courage is not the absence of fear. Courage is when you choose to acknowledge your fear and look it in the face.

What are you afraid of? Everyone is afraid of something. Are you afraid of failure? Afraid of what might happen if everyone knew that you, Mr. Perfect, got an F in Science? Are you afraid you might be shunned if everyone knew that your parents were divorced, or your dad was an alcoholic, or you're not really what you say you are? What are you afraid of? If you don't face your fear head-on, it will never go away.

Often, it's our fear that keeps us where we are and prevents us from getting close to God and to others. God can use our fear to remind us of our need for him. We need to forget about ourselves and focus on others. If you have a fear of the unknown, go on a mission trip to a country where you've never been. If you are afraid of failure, try something new that you may not be good at. It's important to acknowledge and confront our fears so we can move past them.

Breaking free from fear is one of the most liberating feelings in the world. By liberating yourself from fear, you open the door of your mind, allowing the room once occupied by fear to be filled with creativity and passion. And when creativity and passion come in and clean things out, you are able to care about more than yourself and your own fears. And that is a good thing.

> "Be strong and courageous. Do not be afraid; do not be discouraged, for the Lord your God will be with you wherever you go."

Joshua 1:9

The Amazing Change

Courage In Action

Whom do you know that is courageous? How do you think they got that way?

Do you think courageous people are afraid of anything? If so, how do you think they deal with it?

Have you ever had to push past a fear? How did you do it?

How would your life be different if you were more courageous?

Isaiah 41:10 says, "So do not fear, for I am with you; do not be dismayed, for I am your God. I will strengthen you and help you; I will uphold you with my righteous right hand." If we trust in this promise, how will it change us?

Courage

Be the Change!

On back of the title page for this chapter, list two things you are afraid might happen. Then list the worst things that could happen if these greatest fears came true. Ask yourself if God would still be the same. The assurance God will be with you could change the way you approach the fear.

Have a talk with God and ask him to help you release your fears to his care.

Find someone you can trust, like a parent or youth pastor whom you can share those fears with and who will pray for you.

LEADERSHIP

"I LONG TO ACCOMPLISH A GREAT AND NOBLE TASK, BUT IT IS MY CHIEF DUTY TO ACCOMPLISH HUMBLE TASKS AS THOUGH THEY WERE GREAT AND NOBLE. THE WORLD IS MOVED ALONG, NOT ONLY BY THE MIGHTY SHOVES OF ITS HEROES, BUT ALSO BY THE AGGREGATE OF THE TINY PUSHES OF EACH HONEST WORKER."

Helen Keller (1880–1968)
Author and disability-rights activist

Take a Look at Leadership

Winston Churchill

Winston Churchill was one of the most important leaders in modern British history — an influential politician, statesman, and author. But what really made him a good leader? Many admire his characteristic wit and wisdom. I've always appreciated his stubborn refusal to give up and his willingness to do the right thing (even when that was difficult). Churchill had some significant flaws — but that's how we all are. There's always room to grow and improve, and we can't wait until we get ourselves straightened out to try to make a difference. I think God can use us even with our weaknesses.

Winston Churchill was born into a fairly wealthy English family in the late 1800s. He got into politics as a young man, and was committed to changing things from the very beginning. He said, "The pessimist sees difficulty in every opportunity. The optimist sees the opportunity in every difficulty." We could use more people like him today: confident, unafraid, and still having a good sense of humor. He was once seated with Lady Nancy Astor when she said to him, "Winston, if I were your wife I would put poison in your coffee." To which he replied, "Nancy, if I were your husband, I'd drink it."

Many believe Churchill had a mild stuttering problem when he was younger, which may have made public speaking hard for

> "What we are required to do now is stand erect and look the world in the face and do our duty without fear or fervor."
>
> **Winston Churchill**

him. Yet he overcame whatever problems he had with the stutter and became one of the most motivational and inspirational speakers in history.

That reminds me of the story of Moses, who was called by God to lead his people out of Egyptian captivity. Moses didn't think he was the best choice for the job and told God he was "slow of speech and tongue" (Exodus 4:10). He even asked God to send someone else. But God equipped him and sent help—in the form of Moses' brother, Aaron—and Moses became a great leader of God's people.

Churchill also had a problem with alcohol. He drank too much, and this could have been very costly as he sought to lead Parliament and the country. If he could have been honest with himself and overcome this problem, perhaps he could have accomplished even greater things.

Nevertheless, Churchill was a good leader whom people wanted to follow. He was wise and didn't hold his influential position over people's heads. That is the kind of leader I want to be. I also want to overcome my challenges with God's help so I can encourage others and avoid causing anyone else to stumble.

Another Look at Leadership

Rakesh

I was reading some modern slave stories when I came across the story of a boy named Rakesh who lived in a village in India. He was sold into slavery by his own parents to pay off a debt.

Consider what that must have been like! If your parents got into financial trouble, they could probably get another mortgage on the house, sell some household items or a car, or borrow money from a family member or friend. Can you imagine parents actually selling their own kid into slavery to take care of a debt? If that happened to you, imagine how you'd feel about yourself and the value you had to your family.

Rakesh and many other children worked in a place where yarn was woven into rugs that were exported to wealthier countries like the United States. The kids were forced to weave rugs all day, squatting down with their backs against the wall. They didn't go to school. They didn't play with friends. They didn't enjoy the freedoms we take for granted. The slave masters wanted children because they have little fingers that can weave the intricate patterns that bring a lot of money in rug stores.

Let me make Rakesh's life plain: It's not like he was working at a job he just didn't like. Or had a weekend job where his boss wasn't nice. If Rakesh didn't show up to work on time, he was beaten with the iron claw used to separate threads. The claw was a heavy metal device with teeth (like a comb's) on one end and a curved handle on the other end.

Rakesh worked in this situation for a long time until an organization called Free the Slaves joined with local rescuers to free Rakesh and the other children. (For more info, visit www. freetheslaves.com.) The rescuers built little thatched schools for the freed children where they could learn to read and write and begin to build a brighter future. Rakesh is now head of the disciplinary committee at his school. If students get in a fight, he calls them to the front of the classroom and makes them apologize. He says, "You were beaten before by your slave master. Take advantage of this opportunity to make something of yourselves." Kind of ironic, isn't it? God took this young slave boy and gave him a leadership position. It reminds me of the Bible story of Joseph, whose brothers sold him into slavery, but God honored him by putting him in leadership. God has a way of using unlikely people to do great things, and he can take a bad situation and turn it into good.

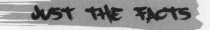

JUST THE FACTS

50: Percentage of all victims of human trafficking that are children

Sources: U.S. House of Representatives Committee on International Relations and U.S. Department of State, among others

What about You?

Living Out Leadership Today

Many of us think we'll make a difference "someday." It seems like we often live for "someday." We think things will be better next semester. Or it'll be easier when we make it to the next grade. Or we'll be happier if we just had more money or a nicer house. But I think God wants us to live for him today—not just wait for "someday."

Throughout history God has used kids to accomplish his purposes. Think about David—too young and too small for a job bigger and older men had turned down. Men would have passed him by, but God used him to slay a giant. Or what about Mary? She was just a teenager, but God chose her to be the mother of Jesus. God could have chosen Elizabeth—someone older and more experienced who really wanted to be a mother. Certainly Elizabeth would have been more qualified by the local gossipers' standards. But Mary was God's choice. And what about the kid with the sack lunch? Instead of having the disciples go fishing or providing food for the massive crowd in another way, Jesus decided to share the lunch of a young boy with a crowd of five thousand.

I think God is still about using kids and proving to the world he is the one who decides the abilities and usefulness of people. Take my friend Leeland—a guy who started writing songs and leading his congregation in worship when he was just a kid. He's being used to lead a whole new generation in getting closer to God through worship and praise. God didn't check Leeland's ID to make sure he was old enough. God used him because Lee was willing, available, and passionate.

So if you're thinking God has to wait for "someday" to use you, think again. God wants to use you *right now*. You can be a leader in your sphere of influence. You can lead in your school by speaking up when someone's being mistreated, or remaining silent when you're tempted to say something derogatory or hurtful. You can lead by befriending kids who are having a tough time, or not becoming arrogant or creating a clique because of your popularity. You can lead by setting a good example of character and solid morals by abstaining from sex and substances that harm your body. The qualities of a good leader are discernment (knowing when enough is enough), wisdom (applying biblical truth to everyday situations), confidence (not cockiness), and determination (stick-to-itiveness).

The Bible doesn't say you need to be a certain age to be a leader. In fact, 1 Timothy 4:12 says, "Don't let anyone look down on you because you are young, but set an example for the believers in speech, in conduct, in love, in faith and in purity." Pretty amazing that God is saying young people should be the ones who set the example for others. It's important to know also that, as a leader, there is more expected from you. God actually judges leaders more harshly than he judges followers, because they have assumed positions as guides. There might be some junk in your life you need to clean up so you have credibility as a leader. It can help if you have someone older and more mature in your life who can help you deal with those rough spots. If you'll allow this person to be truthful with you about your flaws and weaknesses, and help you encounter God's grace for those areas, you'll grow closer to God in the process. Be willing to learn from those with more experience, so you'll be able to lead others in the right direction.

"Don't let anyone look down on you because you are young, but set an example for the believers in speech, in life, in conduct, in faith and in purity."

I Timothy 4:12

The Amazing Change

Leadership in Action

Have you ever decided not to do something because you thought someone else would?

What do you think you're uniquely qualified to do in serving God and others?

What do you think about the idea of waiting until "someday" to be used, to be happy, to find contentment? Have you experienced this in your own life?

LEADERSHIP

Is there a time when you've felt a prompting from God to do something but didn't because you were afraid of failing or that others would not accept your leadership?

Are there areas of your life you need to clean up with God's help in order to clear the way for leading?

What kind of person do you like to follow? What makes for a good leader?

Leadership

Be the Change!

On the back of the title page for this chapter, list three leadership qualities you have that could be used for God.

Think of a friend of yours whom you admire as a leader. What are three qualities you've observed that make this person a good leader? Tell your friend what you've observed as a way of encouraging them.

Find two or three people who are not being treated fairly, or who have been ostracized for some reason. Ask God to provide you with opportunities to show those people grace and kindness this week. Lead by example.

COMPASSION

"HOW FAR YOU GO IN LIFE DEPENDS ON
YOUR BEING TENDER WITH THE YOUNG,
COMPASSIONATE WITH THE AGED, SYMPATHETIC WITH
THE STRIVING, AND TOLERANT OF THE WEAK
AND STRONG. BECAUSE SOMEDAY IN LIFE,
YOU WILL HAVE BEEN ALL OF THESE."

George Washington Carver (1864-1943)
Inventor, agriculturalist, educator, and former slave

Take a Look at Compassion

George Müller

George Müller (pronounced "myoo-ler") died more than one hundred years ago, but his story is still relevant. His father was fairly influential in their hometown in Germany. But George was one of the "bad kids"—the kind of kid your parents don't want you to hang with. He stole, he drank, and he lied. In fact, the night his mother died (when George was just fourteen), he was out getting drunk and playing cards. Some guy, huh?

George's father sent him off to a university, where he came to know Christ. It was then that George developed a burning passion to do God's will and decided to become a missionary. But the girl he was in love with told him she could never marry a missionary. Her dream was that he'd become an influential preacher with a large church (and a large salary), and they could enjoy a life of luxury.

But it wasn't just his girlfriend who wouldn't stand with him. Even George's father was raging mad when George told him about his passion for the mission field. Mr. Müller told his son he would disown him if he became a missionary. Tough spot.

George was still determined and went to missionary school. He traveled to London and began ministering to Jews there, not knowing if God would ever send him on the mission field. But he was willing to go—even if it meant leaving everyone he loved behind.

BE THE CHANGE

As George grew in his faith, he realized the mission field God had in mind for him was right in front of his face! God wanted him to minister to everyone he met. George fell in love with Mary Groves, a woman who shared his faith in God, his commitment to missions, and his compassion for the poor. After he and Mary were wed, they sold most of their possessions, and George started preaching regularly at a local church. Even though it was a hard time for the Müllers, God never stopped supplying for their needs. Whenever they were out of food, George prayed, and God sent them something to eat. This is "give us this day our daily bread" prayer in action.

George was walking on the street one day when he met a little orphan girl named Emily who was out with her little brother. She asked him for a shilling and then walked off. George realized he had seen hundreds of beggar children like Emily on the street and decided he needed to do something to help them. He felt God tugging at his heartstrings, telling him to help these kids. He decided to start a "Breakfast Club" in which he fed orphans and led them to Christ. The Breakfast Club soon got so large that the Müllers decided to build an orphanage to meet the massive needs. As children kept pouring in, two more orphanages were soon established.

One day, there wasn't enough food to go around. George called all the children to the table, and they prayed together. George thanked God for the food God would provide for them (again, the "daily bread" prayer). As soon as they said amen, there was a knock at the door. The baker who lived near the Müllers had baked two loaves for them the night before, because God told her George Müller needed it. Soon, there was another knock on the door. This time it was the milkman. His cart had broken down right in front of the Müllers' house, and the milk was going to spoil if someone didn't use it. There was enough milk and bread to go around, and they even had enough milk to put in their tea at teatime. How amazing is that?

George and Mary Müller lived their lives filled with compassion for children who were without a home and for people who hadn't yet discovered the joy of a friendship with Jesus. One night, after reading a passage of Scripture as he had done countless times before, George Müller died peacefully in his sleep. But the orphanage didn't die with him. In fact, the George Müller Foundation he established continues to meet the needs of the poor and hurting to this day.

JUST THE FACTS

800,000: Number of persons trafficked across international borders each year

Source: U.S. State Department

Another Look at Compassion

Mother Teresa

Most of us have heard of Mother Teresa, but do we really know who she was? She once described herself in this way: "By blood, I am Albanian. By citizenship, an Indian. By faith, I am a Catholic nun. As to my calling, I belong to the world. As to my heart, I belong entirely to the heart of Jesus." Mother Teresa also said she was "God's pencil—a tiny bit of pencil with which he writes what he likes." I like that. Being a little tool God can use to do practical things and speak for him to others. Some nuns who knew her in her earlier days described her as "quiet and shy." But she overcame her shyness because her focus was on the needs of others. This is compassion.

Agnes Gonxha Bojaxhiu—the woman the world came to know as Mother Teresa—was born in Albania in 1910. Her father was a wealthy construction contractor who died of an unknown cause when Agnes was only eight years old. After this incident, she delved more deeply into spiritual things and, at the age of eighteen, decided to become a nun (proof you can make a difference, no matter how young you are). Even though she could have lived a life of comfort, she chose to give her life to serve God and live without earthly possessions.

After several years of training to become a nun, Mother Teresa went to India to teach at a girls' high school. She spent a

lot of time there, but her conscience was bugging her. Outside
the tall walls of the school, there was so much suffering and
hurting. She wanted to be a part of bringing hope, not just to the
girls who could afford to attend school, but to the people of the
street. So after she finished her time at the school, she hit the
streets of Calcutta.

She started by teaching little children from the slums. She
wanted to teach the children how to read, how to take care of
their bodies and avoid sickness, and, most importantly, how to
know the love of Christ. Wherever she went in Calcutta, she
found suffering; it was a place full of poverty and disease. It
would have been easy for her to get discouraged and give up.
After all, how much compassion can one little woman work up in
the face of so much need?

Despite the overwhelming size of the problems, Mother
Teresa never ceased praying and caring for those in need. But
she wasn't alone in her efforts. Within a year, nuns started coming from all over to help the sick and poor and follow in Mother
Teresa's footsteps. They cared for everyone from little children
to the elderly to those suffering with leprosy.

Over the course of her life, Mother Teresa became known as
a mighty woman—someone who spoke out fearlessly about controversial things if she felt she could help the poor she served.
She was a pillar of compassion and was even recognized for her
work by being awarded the Nobel Peace Prize. She kept going

until she ran out of steam at age eighty-seven on September 5, 1997. She had just finished eating her morning meal and praying when the Lord took her home. I can imagine her walking through the gates of heaven as God smiled down on her and said, "Well done, good and faithful servant!"

What about You?

Living Out Compassion Today

Some time ago I was in Grand Rapids, Michigan, team-teaching with a guy named Steve Carter. Steve had invited me up there to speak with his youth group a couple of times, and we were becoming pretty good friends. Over the years he's showed a lot of confidence in me and has helped me discover that young people like me have something worthwhile to say to the church.

Anyway, Steve was telling me about this new word he'd made up: *wombish*. Before you get weirded out, let me tell you what he means by that. You see, the word *compassion* in the Old Testament is actually the plural form of the word *womb*. So basically, being compassionate is being wombish. The Bible tells us to be compassionate as God is compassionate. When we think of God's compassion as being like a womb, it's a pretty cool picture. A womb is the ultimate safe environment, where virtually nothing can harm you, and the mother must give away a piece of herself in order to keep you safe. As a matter of fact, if the person doing the protecting weren't there, then life in the womb would cease to exist. I think that's the kind of compassion and care we should offer to people who are oppressed and hurting around the world. (And this doesn't apply just to situations as drastic as slavery.)

Steve also pointed out the first few verses of Isaiah 61 to me, in which Isaiah says the Spirit of God is upon him, giving him a mission to preach to the lowest of the low, to break bonds, and to bandage wounds. Jesus reads these very same words aloud as he begins his own ministry (Luke 4:18–19). God sent Isaiah — and Jesus — to reach out to the hurting, the despised, the rejects. And God asks the same of each of us.

Though he's now the senior pastor at my church, my friend Steve lived this out among the youth he ministered to in Michigan. After speaking at the church, I had the opportunity to have pizza with some of the middle and high school kids. Each student around the table shared with me how they were living out compassion in their lives. A group of middle schoolers told me they had learned of some people in their own community who were unable to pay their electric bills and were in danger of living in freezing conditions. The students decided to raise money by recycling cans so they could pay their neighbors' heating bills. Other students went to the region devastated by Katrina and helped with the cleanup. Still others went on short-term missions trips outside the country. It was great to see so many students living out their faith to help others and becoming wombish.

Some people seem to be afraid of an idea they call the "social gospel." I don't know everything they mean by that term, but I think they're concerned that if we emphasize serving the poor and bringing justice as part of God's calling for us, we're saying living for Christ isn't about holiness and trying to get closer to God. But I don't see it that way. Compassion is not some alternate gospel. Compassion is an overflow of the gospel—the Good News of Christ's sacrifice. Compassion says we have embraced the relationship with God through Christ. It's not that we have to earn our salvation by doing good things, but compassion and service flow out of us because we are filled with God's love. If we don't take care of orphans and widows, if we don't care for the poor and hurting, how can we say we belong to Jesus?

"The purpose of life is not to be happy. It is to be useful, to be honorable, to be compassionate, to have it make some difference that you have lived and lived well."

Ralph Waldo Emerson (1803–1882)
Poet and writer

The Amazing Change

Compassion in Action

How do you feel when you learn about deep suffering around the world? Do you feel distant or disconnected from the problems of others? Do you want to plug your ears and not hear any more? Or do you feel drawn to do something about it? Answer honestly!

Even though it's a weird word, think about this word "wombish" for a little while. What do you think it would look like in your life for you to be "wombish" toward people in your school who are suffering? What about people in your larger community — the homeless, fatherless, or sick? What about people who make you feel uncomfortable? What about people around the globe?

Have you ever been involved in serving someone in need? How did it make you feel? How do you think it makes God feel?

Do you think of serving the poor and needy as a way to get to God or as an overflow of the relationship you already have with him?

Check out James 1:27. What does James mean when he talks about "pure religion"?

Compassion

Be the Change!

Consider setting aside a portion of your allowance or salary to help the poor. This would be above and beyond any tithe you might pay to the church.

Spend some time as a volunteer for a service organization in your area. Perhaps you could help serve lunch at a soup kitchen or help out at a hospital.

Think of something practical you can do to help someone in need. Write your idea on the back of the title page for this chapter, and make a plan to do it. Think big! If it's during the winter, you could go out and buy hats, gloves, and heavy socks to donate to a homeless shelter. Or maybe you could buy a secret present to brighten the day of someone who needs a friend. Try one of these ideas or — even better — think outside the box, and come up with your own idea.

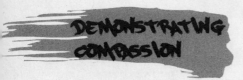

DEMONSTRATING COMPASSION

Many organizations are reaching out to show compassion to the poor. These are some of my favorites:

Compassion International ~ www.Compassion.com

Food for the Hungry ~ www.fh.org

World Vision ~ www.Worldvision.org

Salvation Army ~ www.salvationarmy.org

Association of Gospel Rescue Missions ~ www.agrm.org

ENDURANCE

"WE COULD NEVER LEARN TO BE BRAVE
AND PATIENT IF THERE WERE ONLY
JOY IN THE WORLD."

Helen Keller (1880–1968)
Author and disability-rights activist

Take a Look at Endurance

Jesse Owens

If you ask your parents or grandparents who the best Olympic athlete of all time was, they'll probably say Jesse Owens. In his athletic career, Owens won many medals and awards, and gained a lot of recognition away from the track as well. In fact, President Gerald Ford formally awarded Owens the Medal of Freedom, the highest government honor any civilian (nonsoldier) can receive. But let's start at the beginning of his story.

In 1913, in a little Alabama town, a baby was born to an African American couple named Henry and Emma Owens. They named the baby James Cleveland Owens, but everyone called him "J.C." Henry Owens moved his family up to Cleveland, Ohio before J.C. began school, seeking a better job. On J.C.'s first day of school, his teacher asked his name and thought J.C. said his name was "Jesse." From that point on, everyone called him Jesse.

When Jesse got into high school, his gym teacher noticed he had a lot of potential and started to coach him in running. Jesse got better and better and, while still in high school, ended up tying the world record for the 100-yard dash with a time of 9.4 seconds. Now, all you track athletes out there, imagine running a 100-yard dash in 9.4 seconds! That would be *insane*. But I digress …

Owens became a renowned track star, and colleges started paying attention to his success. Jesse chose to go to The Ohio

State University, but he wasn't allowed to live on the campus because he was black. This is the part of the story where I start to get angry. Even though he was one of the best athletes in the history of the world, when the track team traveled Jesse was forced to sleep in the "colored" hotels and couldn't eat at the "whites-only" restaurants. This was because of the stiff segregation laws in place at the time. This incredibly talented and dedicated young man was viewed only through the lens of color. He experienced degradation day in and day out.

The week before one of Jesse's track meets, he fell down a flight of stairs, severely injuring his back. This injury would plague him for years to come. After receiving treatment he convinced his coach he could run that week in the first of the four events in which he normally competed. After Jesse tied the world record in the 100-yard dash, the coach allowed him to participate in the other three events. When the meet was over, Owens had set new world records in the broad jump, the 200-yard dash, and the 200-yard low hurdles. (In the broad jump, he shattered the previous record by a full six inches!) He was already showing he could overcome obstacles and suffering in order to accomplish his goals. He had the character trait of endurance.

While still in college, Jesse Owens earned a spot on the 1936 U.S. Olympic team. But there's something you should know about those Olympics, which were held that year in Berlin, Germany. During this period of time, Nazi leader Adolf Hitler was trying to take over the world. Hitler presided over these Olympic Games, hoping they would prove to the world that his white German athletes were superior to all other races and nationalities. Jesse proved him wrong by winning four gold medals. He was not only the first African American to win four gold medals in track and field, but the first American ever to do so.

After he retired from running, Owens went on many speaking tours, and started his own public relations firm. Jesse Owens endured the preventable suffering of racism and bigotry, as well as the unpreventable suffering of injury, and succeeded in making his mark on the history of sports and the world.

Another Look at Endurance

David Ngure

A few years ago, I met a young man named David Makara Ngure, who said three words that have had a great impact on me: "Never say die."

If anyone ever had the right to "say die," it was David. He grew up in Kenya as a street kid. A group of Catholic nuns took him in and helped him get an education. As a young man he had a little video business, but still didn't have much money. Yet David had big dreams for his future.

One day David was making a delivery when several corrupt policemen grabbed him and threw him into their car and

"Patience and perseverance have a magical effect before which difficulties disappear and obstacles vanish."

John Quincy Adams (1767–1848)
U.S. president

demanded money from him. A series of events unfolded, which ended in David receiving several gunshot wounds. He was taken to the hospital, where he had to have his hand and part of his arm amputated. The police tried to cover their guilt by framing him for a crime he didn't commit. David was arrested and chained to his hospital bed, and later sent to jail where he was facing a death sentence—all for being in the wrong place at the wrong time.

I can't imagine how afraid he must have been through these events. First, he was abducted, threatened, and shot. Then in the hospital, in tremendous pain, chained to the bed, and about to lose his arm. And later in jail, still suffering greatly, and fearing for his life. Thankfully, attorneys from a nonprofit organization called International Justice Mission heard about his case and were not only able to clear David of the charges but even made sure the police were arrested for their crimes. That is the strong hand of justice!

On the day I met David, he was teaching in a chapel service at my school. In front of the whole high school, he told the whole story of his kidnapping, hospitalization, arrest, imprisonment, and release. But in the middle of it he stopped and started singing a song he'd written while he was in prison. When he translated the words for us, it reminded me of the verses in Job in which Job says, "Though he slay me, yet will I hope in him." It was a song of enduring hope. Of enduring trust in God. Of a man who was willing to endure suffering because he believed God loved him.

After David finished teaching and the room cleared out, I walked over to thank him for coming. He looked me in the eye, and I got the feeling what he was about to say was very important. He told me he believed God had big plans for me and that he was proud of me for speaking up for the oppressed. He also said he would rather not have his hand and serve God than to have his hand and be living his own way. That blew me away— that he could view his amputation in this way and not be bitter toward God. He also encouraged me to follow hard after God, reminding me of the verse in 1 Timothy that says, "Don't let anyone look down on you because you are young" (4:12).

Even though David has suffered a lot, he is a great encourager. He loves life. David is an amazing man who has returned to Kenya, where he has begun the long process of getting a law degree so he can advocate for others who are oppressed.

JUST THE FACTS

$16.4 Million: U.S. government budget for grant making efforts against human trafficking

Source: U.S. State Department

$19 Billion: U.S. government budget for efforts against drug trafficking

Source: White House drug policy website

What about You?

Living Out Endurance Today

Have you ever had a bad day? Most of us think we have. You might feel like you're having a bad day because friends are gossiping about you or something happened in English class. Or maybe it's when your big game gets cancelled because of rain, or you get a bad grade in Science and are told you can't play Xbox. But that's not a bad day.

For many people around the world, a truly bad day is when you wake up to the sound of your slave master yelling at you, telling you to get to work. You get off the hard ground you slept on, still sore from last night's beatings. Quickly, you wash the dust off yourself, and eat a hurried breakfast of rice and water. You make it to your workplace on time; if you don't, you are beaten severely. Then you crouch on the floor with the other slaves, your backs pressed against the walls in a dark, dusty, smelly room, weaving rugs all day long. Then you go to sleep, and repeat the process the next morning. This is the life of a slave.

This story isn't intended to make you feel guilty (although it might), but it is intended to make you think. I know some of us do suffer greatly, and I don't mean to minimize that. Some kids have to endure the loss of someone they love, the divorce of parents, or the suffering of a terminal illness. I don't want to minimize how difficult these experiences can be. But how many of us complain about little things each day—our lunches, our hair, our homework, our clothes, our friends, our teammates, or our family members? I'd say most of us do. And I think that is wrong.

We shouldn't complain about every little thing that doesn't go our way. Or the petty things that bug us about others. If your looks or your clothes bother you, pray God would make you thankful you have clothes to wear. If you're upset about some-thing at school, be thankful you have the chance to go to school, get an education, and visit with friends instead of weaving rugs all day. If people in your life annoy you, pray for them too! That person who's bugging you? Ask God to let you see him as God sees him, or love her as God loves her.

We should all be thankful for how much we have been given. We can become obsessed with comparing ourselves with others—whether it's to brag about how much better we are than "them" or to be jealous of what someone else has that we don't. Instead, why don't we try comparing ourselves with people like modern-day slaves and the oppressed? We'll probably find we have it pretty good in comparison. Thankfully, most of us will never have to know the kind of suffering and hardship slaves endure every day.

I think it's really cool that God chooses to use us to alleviate suffering. God hears the cries of the oppressed. If we open our hearts, we can be the answer to their cries for relief and hope, so their enduring will not be in vain.

"Many of life's failures are men who did not realize how close they were to success when they gave up."

Thomas Edison (1847–1931)
Scientist and inventor

The Amazing Change

Endurance in Action

What does it mean to endure? What can help a person endure great hardship?

What kind of thoughts do you think were running through David's head while he was in the hospital and in jail? Where do you think God was while David was enduring these struggles?

How do you think God wants to use us to bring relief from suffering?

Has anyone close to you ever suffered greatly? How did it make you feel? What lengths would you have gone to in order to alleviate that person's suffering?

How do you feel when you learn that children and entire families are still being held as slaves and that innocent people like David are oppressed? What are these feelings telling you to do?

Read Proverbs 31:8–9. How do you see yourself living out those verses?

Endurance

Be the Change!

On the back of the title page for this chapter, write a journal entry pretending you are David Ngure or Jesse Owens. Describe how you feel about the suffering and oppression you're experiencing.

Pray God would give you compassion for people who are suffering—especially people who are not like you.

Ask God to prevent oppressors from hurting innocent people. And pray God might give those who are suffering the strength to endure.

Tell someone the story of David Ngure or Jesse Owens today. Inspire them to live out Proverbs 31:8–9.

SACRIFICE

"IN THIS WORLD
IT IS NOT WHAT WE TAKE UP,
BUT WHAT WE GIVE UP,
THAT MAKES US RICH."

Henry Ward Beecher (1813–1887)
Pastor and social reformer

Take a Look at Sacrifice

John Rankin

You're running through the woods, the shouts of your pursuers close behind you. Your basic human instinct overrides all else: survival! As you run through the forest, you lift your arms in front of your face to keep from losing an eye to a tree branch. That happened to Aunt Martha. Or at least they said it did; after she tried to escape and run to the North, no one knew what became of her. Some said she drowned in the river. Others said she was caught, sold, and taken down to Alabama.

Faster ... faster, you feel as though you can't run anymore, but you must. Your legs now have no feeling, and your arms are scraped and bleeding. You must survive. You hear the hounds getting closer as you come to the bank of the misty Ohio River. In the darkness it appears motionless, but you've heard tales of people sinking down into the thick, brown mud at the bottom, as if being swallowed whole. You try to put that out of your mind as you take your first steps into the water. You are so thirsty. Your throat is so parched it burns like fire when you swallow, and your tongue is so dry it sticks to the roof of your mouth. Still the instinct to survive propels you on.

Freedom. You turn the word over in your head as your pursuers hear you splashing and start to fire their guns. You swim furiously across the river, knowing one of the stray bullets peppering the water behind you might find its mark at any moment. Failure is not an option. Giving up would mean death or worse. You can't go back to the beatings, the humiliation of being treated like an animal—*you can't!*

You make it to the other side, but farther down the bank you hear a raft coming ashore, and the piercing shots that could come only from a rifle. The gut-wrenching racket draws nearer. Surrender enters your mind, but quickly exits as the mantra of freedom beats in your head. You sprint with newfound energy through the field of tall grass that reaches up a large hill like a spectral, green hand. You run through the grass, trying to make as little noise as possible, slowed by your soaked clothes.

Survival! Freedom! Pounding with your pulse. You pause for just a moment to glance over your shoulder at where the slave catchers were last. You can still see their hats, and hear the baying of their hounds. You finally reach the top of the hill, but you are not safe.

What if there is no candle? You almost sob at the thought. *What if I crossed at the wrong part of the river?* You almost faint from fear and sorrow, but then you see it in the window of the stately home. The candle. Freedom. You run to the door and pound on it with your last ounce of strength. The door opens and a strong hand pulls you quickly inside. You are taken into a back bedroom where a thin section of floorboards is lifted up and you are directed to climb inside.

SACRIFICE

Above, you hear the slave catchers arrive at the door and demand to be shown through the house. They move from room to room loudly; it doesn't matter if you're snuck up on. An escaped slave shot dead is worth the same reward. They move to the room where you are lying. Your heart pounds so loud you are sure the catchers can hear it. Then it happens. You breathe in just a little and sneeze. It's loud enough to wake the dead, but luckily — no, luck has nothing to do with it — one of the hounds steps on a splinter and yelps at the same time as your giveaway sneeze. The slave catchers leave the home of John Rankin empty-handed, and you are safe for one more night. Thus ends the first chapter of freedom in the life of a runaway slave.

John Rankin knew all about fugitive slaves. In fact, he spent his entire life saving theirs. He and his wife and their thirteen children lived for the majority of their lives in a house that was home not just to a large family, but also to some much-sought-after house guests.

The Rankin house was in Ripley, Ohio, located on a three-hundred-foot hill overlooking the Ohio River. The location of this home made it an ideal hiding place for runaway slaves. The Ohio River was one of the only natural barriers keeping slaves from escaping to the North. In order to signal that it was safe to cross the river, Rankin, like many others on the Underground Railroad, would put a lantern or candle in one of his windows.

While helping runaway slaves was never easy, it became even harder when the Fugitive Slave Act of 1850 was passed. This act declared even slaves who made it to the "Free North" could still be captured and taken back to their masters in the South. Even though the odds were against him, John Rankin didn't give up. He housed and fed an estimated two thousand people through his stop on the Underground Railroad. Many of their stories may have been like the one you just read. At one point, a $2,500 reward was offered for John Rankin's life, but he and his children guarded the house and its precious visitors tenaciously, risking their own lives to save others.

Despite all the times Rankin's house was searched, despite the thousands of slaves who were hidden there over many years, not a single slave was ever found and recaptured there, because

"Action springs not from thought, but from a readiness for responsibility."

Dietrich Bonhoeffer (1906 – 1945)
German pastor, theologican, and author

Rankin and his sons were more determined than the slave hunters. This is truly amazing, since the slave catchers usually had hounds with them to sniff out slaves.

John Rankin lived a full life as a true hero—a person who was willing to risk his life to save another. And there is truly no greater love than this.

Another Look at Sacrifice

Father and Son

I recently read about a father-son team that runs in marathons, competes in triathlons, and once even made the 3,735 miles across the USA on foot. They're known as Team Hoyt—the dad's name is Dick Hoyt and his son is Rick. Oh, by the way, Rick can't walk or talk. When he was being born, his umbilical cord got wrapped around his neck, cutting off the oxygen to his brain. Doctors told Dick and his wife their son would always be "a vegetable."

But Rick's parents struggled to give him the normal life most of us take for granted. Even things that most of us don't like to do, like walking the dog, were impossible for Rick to do. Rick's mom and dad managed to get him into a public school with a little help from a computer Rick can control with small movements of his head. By using this computer, Rick can convey his thoughts and emotions on the computer screen. (By the way, as a big hockey fan in Massachusetts, Rick's first words were "Go Bruins!")

When Rick was fifteen years old, he asked his dad to participate in a five-mile run with him in order to benefit a local athlete who had been paralyzed in an accident. Dick was not a runner—or even an athlete—but he agreed to push Rick through the race in his wheelchair.

Since then, the father-son team has competed in more than nine hundred events together! That includes 10Ks, half-marathons, marathons, and triathlons. For the Ironman Triathlon in Hawaii, which starts with a 2.4-mile ocean swim, Dick puts Rick in a raft and pulls him with a rope tied around his waist. Then he gets out and carries Rick to the start of the 110-mile bike race, where Rick sits in front of his dad on a specially made seat. When they complete that part of the race, Rick is placed in a lightweight wheelchair that Dick pushes for the 26.2 miles of a full marathon. Their best time in this event is 13 hours, 43 minutes, and 37 seconds. I don't understand how anyone can do this without dying!

But hope for a productive, happy life for his son is why Dick began his competitive pursuits. Just think about how huge the commitment is on Dick's part. He gives so much for and to his son. For years, he has worked out and trained—sometimes five hours a day, even when he was working—to stay in shape for the races. Together, the father-son team is a lot like the body of Christ.

"Rick couldn't compete without his dad. Dick wouldn't compete without his son. Dick is the body. Rick is the heart. Together they run."

From *Together: Team Hoyt*, a short movie about the family

What are you and I willing to do for the good of others? How much of ourselves are we willing to give?

What about You?

Living Out Sacrifice Today

If you asked many teens today what *sacrifice* is, they may not even know how to respond. Maybe they'd say it's when someone kills an animal and burns it as an offering to God—an Old Testament example of sacrifice. But that's not the kind of sacrifice I'm talking about. I'm talking about when you give up something of yourself for someone else. I think many young people in America have a hard time understanding what sacrifice is, because in our own world, in our comfortable lives, we don't have many readily available opportunities to sacrifice.

We are a generation that knows its rights. We have had this drilled into us through our education. We have the right to speak our mind, the right to be treated fairly, and the right to be respected. Don't get me wrong; it's great to live in a country where our rights are protected. But we sometimes act as if we have the right to be completely comfortable and maintain whatever is ours, with no care to what others might be going through. The question is: Are we willing to make any sacrifices in order to benefit someone else?

Let's make it plain. You're fifteen. You've grown up in the same community at the same school with (mostly) the same friends. You're pretty popular, and you know it. I don't mean that in an arrogant way, but you enjoy a good reputation and are respected. Sophomore year starts and a new kid comes to your school. He's looking for a place to sit at lunch. More importantly, he's looking for a place to belong. You have a choice to make. Do you invite him over, even though he might be a threat to your position? Do you sacrifice your comfort and help him get to know other kids? Or do you shut him out?

Or, how about this: It's time for homecoming. You're a senior girl and you've bought a dress you love. It looks great on you, and you're excited for the big night. Your family is having dinner with another family from your school. They have a daughter

who isn't very popular. She's a little shy and has trouble fitting in.
Homecoming is her first big event. Her mom suggests she show
you her dress. You go into her room, she opens her closet and
… there's *your* dress! The one you love so much. She bought the
same one! You have a choice to make. Of course, you have a
right to wear the dress you've been planning to wear. But would
you consider returning it and wearing something else so this
girl can enjoy her big night? Or do you wear the dress and up-
stage her?

These are not life-or-death sacrifices. But they do require
that we lay aside something that matters to us. A sacrifice isn't
just giving someone something. It's giving up something you may
want or need or something that is very important to you.

Also, there are some things we view as our rights that really aren't. We have the right to speak our minds, but does that
mean we always should really say whatever is on our minds? Do
we have the right to hurt people with our words just because
they're true? As Christians we are to lay down our self-interest
and consider others more important than ourselves. This is so
different from our culture and what we usually feel in our hearts.
But if we're to follow the example Jesus set for us, sacrifice for
others can't be dismissed. Remember, too, Jesus didn't consider
the idea of how much we love him or how faithfully we lived
when he decided to give up his life for us. He died for all of us —
the whole big messy world.

"Do nothing out of selfish ambition or vain conceit. Rather, in humility consider others above yourselves."

Philippians 2:3

The Amazing Change

Sacrifice in Action

What is sacrifice? What does it look like today?

What is selfishness? What does it look like today?

SACRIFICE

What would it look like if we were "selfless"?

What does Philippians 2:3 mean when it says we should consider others above ourselves?

Do you think our generation has lost the ability to be humble and put others first? What would you be willing to sacrifice for someone else? For whom would you make that sacrifice?

Should we make sacrifices only to benefit those closest to us? What do you think of the idea of not allowing distance to determine our willingness to sacrifice and show compassion?

Sacrifice

Be the Change!

Consider following the tradition of the Underground Railroad by putting an electric candle in your window as a reminder that you want to stand for freedom from oppression and be a voice for the voiceless.

Go to **www.nurfc.org** to learn more about the Underground Railroad and modern-day slavery.

Check out the final section of this book to learn more about Loose Change to Loosen Chains and see how you can be part of ending slavery today. On the back of the title page for this chapter, write down at least one thing you will do to make a difference.

OVERCOMING

"i am not afraid of storms,
for i'm learning
to sail my ship."

Louisa May Alcott (1832–1888)
Author and abolitionist

Take a Look at Overcoming

Olaudah Equiano

Olaudah Equiano, a slave in the 1700s, traveled an unusual path toward freedom—a path that showed his ability to overcome the great injustice suffered by thousands of slaves during his time in history.

Equiano was born in Nigeria, but was separated from his parents and taken into captivity at age eleven. Eventually, he was sold to an officer in England's Royal Navy named Michael Pascal. Although Equiano's experience as a naval slave was certainly not easy, he was able to avoid many of the most difficult elements of being a slave on plantations. In fact, Pascal even sent him to a school in London where Equiano learned to read and write. This would prove to be a great advantage to Equiano throughout his life.

After serving Pascal on board a warship, Equiano was sold to another sea captain, who took him to the Caribbean and sold him once again to a Quaker merchant named Robert King. Because of his education, Equiano was not sent to the plantation fields and avoided the horrible, torturous treatment that other slaves faced. Instead, his job was to weigh and measure the products produced on the plantation—sort of a quality-control job. But witnessing the plight of his fellow slaves made Olaudah Equiano all the more intent on securing his own freedom.

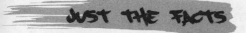

218 Million: Estimated number of children working between ages five and seventeen

126 Million: Estimated number of children who work in the worst forms of child labor (one in every twelve children ages five to seventeen)

Sources: International Labor Organization, UNICEF, and U.S. Embassy in Uruguay, among others

He asked King what it would cost to buy his freedom. King said he would sell Equiano his freedom for the same price he had paid when he purchased the slave—forty pounds. By selling and trading with other merchants, Equiano was able to buy his freedom after only three years.

He went on to write his autobiography, which became a bestseller in England and brought attention to the conditions that slaves faced. Sales of his book made Equiano a wealthy man. He then used his influence to add his voice to the opposition of the slave trade in Great Britain. Although he died before Parliament passed the ban on slavery, Equiano definitely brought a new face and voice to the plight of slaves during that battle for freedom.

Equiano's life was complicated and diverse—from the beauty and peace of his early childhood in Africa to his kidnapping and removal from all that was familiar; from his job aboard a warship to his sale and resale like an animal or a piece of equipment. Even with all the uncertainty that came with being owned by someone else (and, therefore, at their mercy), Equiano overcame the unfairness and treachery of slavery and eventually helped many others win their freedom.

Another Look at Overcoming

Given Kachepa

Not long ago, I was in Washington, D.C. to meet with some other people who are working to abolish modern-day slavery. I met Ambassador John Miller, who then headed up the State Department's office to fight human trafficking, as well as a congressman and several other leaders from Capitol Hill. But the person who most impressed me was a young man not much older than me. His name is Given Kachepa. He's about 5'6" with dark skin and eyes that display kindness and goodness. If you met Given, you'd never guess that his story is one of pain and struggle. You'd never guess that at age eleven Given became a slave.

Given was born in Zambia, a country in the southern part of Africa. Life wasn't easy for him from the start. While he was still in elementary school in Zambia, both his parents died—first his mother, then his father. People who take part in human trafficking and owning slaves often prey on orphans, because they have no one to take care of them or look out for them. In fact, most oppressors are cowards who take advantage of those who are most vulnerable.

Like many other young people, Given was tricked into slavery. It happened shortly after he finished the seventh grade. A ministry called TTT announced it was funding tours for the Zambian Boys Choir. Given went to the auditions and was one of twelve boys selected to join the choir. Given practiced for two years with the group before coming to America. The boys were all promised that the money they made from singing in churches would go to build schools in Zambia, and that some of it would be sent back to their families. They were also promised they would receive two full bags of clothes, baptism, an education, and "a great reward" at the end of the tour. None of these promises was kept. When any of the boys asked about money or schooling, they were told to concentrate on singing and not be so selfish. The boys traveled around the country in a small van, got little sleep, and often had to sing up to twenty times a week. I can't even begin to imagine being cooped up in a van like that on long road trips. Imagine having to wake up at four o' clock in the morning day after day, knowing you have another full day of singing and traveling ahead of you—and you're just a kid. The boys were also forced to do all of their own cooking and cleaning, and most of them weren't even in their teens.

One time, Given and the other boys refused to sing, so the

leader of TTT unplugged the gas stove where they were staying. Those were the rules: no singing, no food. Given and the other boys were afraid *not* to sing because they might be sent back to Zambia.

We might wonder, "Why didn't Given just try to get sent back to Zambia?" Well, this might seem like a good idea to us, but for those Zambian boys, getting sent back would have suggested they had done something to disgrace their families—and they would basically be excommunicated. In his culture, there were consequences for shaming your family name.

Eventually, a government agency started looking into the situation, after being tipped off by some people from churches where the boys had sung. One by one the agency took boys away from TTT and put them safely into loving foster homes. An investigation revealed that the leaders of TTT were using the boys as virtual slaves, and the money they had promised would be used to build a school, provide for their families, and strengthen their community in Zambia was just being pocketed by the TTT leaders.

Given has been emancipated from slavery and grew up with his American family, the Shepards. He's now attending dental school in Texas and recently returned to Zambia to visit the members of his family who are still living. Given has overcome so much and is an inspiration to others. He's an incredible guy with lots of tenacity and strength.

What about You?

Living Out Overcoming Today

If you talk to just about any respected leader, you probably find this person has faced some significant challenges at some point in life. In fact, I think everyone has some kind of challenge to overcome. It might be a learning disability or a difficult family situation. Or maybe it's an abusive parent or a financial struggle. Perhaps you move and have to start all over with the challenge of being "the new kid." Maybe you're from a different race or culture than most kids in your school, or your family has different standards. Any of these can create obstacles that can get in the way of your success. But they can also be seen as challenges we can overcome with God's help.

Sometimes we want to run away from our challenges and weaknesses. How great would it be if we could look at our weaknesses as a chance to get closer to Jesus? Paul found this secret after he had complained many times to God about a weakness he had. He says in 2 Corinthians that God told him:

> My grace is enough; it's all you need. My strength comes into its own in your weakness. Once I heard that, I was glad to let it happen. I quit focusing on the handicap and began appreciating the gift. It was a case of Christ's strength moving in on my weakness. Now I take limitations in stride, and with good

*cheer, these limitations that cut me down to size — abuse,
accidents, opposition, bad breaks. I just let Christ take over!
And so the weaker I get, the stronger I become.*

2 Corinthians 12:9 - 10, *The Message*

The Bible reminds us God is with us through all our struggles. Jeremiah 29:11 reads: "'For I know the plans I have for you,' declares the Lord, 'plans to prosper you and not to harm you, plans to give you hope and a future.'" And sometimes the obstacles we have to overcome can make us stronger, helping us live into that hopeful future that God has placed before us.

The Amazing Change

Overcoming in Action

What challenges do you have to overcome in your life? Are you facing an obstacle that seems too big for you alone? What does that problem look like right now?

Think of a few words that describe how you're feeling about the challenges you face. As you consider these feelings, remember that God is with you through your struggles.

Olaudah Equiano and Given Kachepa had plenty of reasons to be bitter and angry. How would their lives have been different if they had let bitterness rule in their hearts?

In what ways are you like Olaudah or Given? How are you different from them? In what ways do you wish you were more like them?

Maybe things are pretty sweet right now, and you don't see any big challenges awaiting you in the near future. If that's the case, this is a good time to get strong and prepare for rough times ahead. We know for sure we'll have things to overcome—Scripture makes that pretty clear. But remember these words from Jesus: "In this world, you will have trouble. But take heart! I have overcome the world" (John 16:33).

Overcoming

Be the Change!

Think of someone you know who is currently facing something they need to overcome. How can you help that person go through this time?

You might send an email, instant message, or card to let them know you care about them. Or maybe you need to offer some practical help to lighten their load. What do you plan to do?

On the back of the title page for this chapter, write a quick note to your friend—just a sentence or two. Don't try to fix the problem—just let your friend know you care. Tear out that page and give it to your friend.

STANDING FIRM

"BE SURE YOU PUT YOUR FEET
IN THE RIGHT PLACE,
THEN STAND FIRM."

Abraham Lincoln (1809-1865)
U.S. president and abolitionist

Take a Look at Standing Firm

Two Cousins and Three Vegans

The Bible is filled with people who dared to stand up for what was right. Have you ever read the book of Esther? If you haven't, you should. It's a story of love, hate, suspense, and a conspiracy to wipe out an entire race of people. It also has a great ending: The hero wins. In this case the hero (actually, the heroine) is an orphan girl named Esther.

Esther was living with her older cousin Mordecai in Persia when word spread that the queen had been dethroned, and the king was now looking for a new queen. Young women from all over Persia were summoned to appear before the king. Esther was chosen to be one of them.

Her real name wasn't Esther, though; her real name was Hadassah. Mordecai had told her to change it so no one would know she was a Jew.

When Esther arrived at the palace, she didn't get to see the king right away. She and all the other girls went through an EXTREME makeover—more than twelve months of beauty treatment! About half the time was spent on perfume; the other half on makeup. That's some serious mirror time and a pretty amazing spa package! When it was Esther's turn to see the king, she charmed him more than any of the other girls, and she won the crown. Fast forward a little bit ...

BE THE CHANGE

One day, as Esther's cousin Mordecai was sitting at the castle gates, he overheard two of the guards plotting the assassination of the king. Mordecai ran and told his cousin, Queen Esther, who in turn reported it to the king, giving credit to Mordecai. When the report was verified, the two guards were hanged. At the same time the king was showing more and more favor to an advisor named Haman. Eventually, Haman rose to a powerful position, second only to the king. Haman was very proud, and required that everyone bow to him. Everyone did — except for one guy. Mordecai refused to bow to anyone but his own God.

When Haman found out Mordecai was Jewish, he persuaded the king to have all Jews destroyed, saying they were rebellious, lawless people. When Mordecai told Esther what Haman was planning to do, she was scared. Mordecai told her, "If you remain silent at this time, relief and deliverance for the Jews will arise from another place, but you and your father's family will perish. And who knows but that you have come to your royal position for such a time as this?" To which Esther replied, "If I perish, I perish!"

About that time, the king couldn't sleep one night, so he had the history of his reign read to him. When the reader came to the part about Mordecai's rescuing the king from assassination, the king said, "Wait a minute! Did I ever do anything to reward this Mordecai for saving my life? I need to do something for that guy."

At that point Esther went to the king and told him, after several attempts, that Haman was trying to kill all Jews — including

Mordecai, Queen Esther herself, and all their people. The king got angry and Haman was hanged on the gallows he had been building to hang Mordecai. Now every year during the Jewish holiday of Purim, Esther and Mordecai are celebrated for their courage in standing firm for what they believed in.

But Esther's not the only example. Have you heard the one about the three vegans? Really, it's not a joke. It's the story of these three teenage guys who were kidnapped and taken to an unfamiliar country called Babylon. Eventually, these three guys — Shadrach, Meshach, and Abednego — ended up in training to become servants of the king, who was named Nebuchadnezzar. (*Man*, they had strange names back then!)

One day, one of the king's attendants tried to get them to drink wine and eat meat. But Shadrach, Meshach, and Abednego had made a vow to God they would not eat meat or drink wine. So they refused. In fact, they issued a challenge to the king's worker — they would eat only vegetables and water for ten days, and the other guys could eat meat and drink wine, and then they'd see who was the strongest. (Sounds kind of like a reality TV challenge!) But Shad, Mesh, and Abed believed God would honor their commitment and dedication by keeping them strong.

Well, when the ten days were up, the three guys were visibly stronger and healthier looking than all of the others. Everyone was amazed these vegans were looking so good! So the three young men were brought in to serve the king.

But their trouble wasn't over. King Neb had a giant gold statue made and issued an order that when his royal musicians played, everyone was to bow down and worship the statue. When the music started, all the king's subjects fell down and started worshiping the statue—except for Shad, Mesh, and Abed, who weren't bowing down. Some astrologers went to the king and ratted on the guys, probably because they were jealous the three teens had such great jobs.

King Neb had the guys brought in and asked them if it was true they had not followed his orders. They explained they would worship only God. King Neb was furious and demanded they be thrown in a furnace. These young men stood firm and said, "We do not need to defend ourselves before you in this matter. If we are thrown into the blazing furnace, the God we serve is able to deliver us from it, and he will deliver us from Your Majesty's hand. But even if he does not, we want you to know, Your Majesty, that we will not serve your gods or worship the image of gold you have set up" (Daniel 3:16-18).

These guys had a pretty incredible faith. It's hard enough to stand up for what you believe when you might face ridicule. But these must have been some pretty radical dudes to stand firm when their lives were on the line.

Their commitment paid off—you probably know the story already. The king had the furnace turned up seven times hotter than usual. He was ticked. When the guys were tied up and tossed in, the furnace was so hot that workers who threw the guys in died from its heat. But the flames didn't burn Shadrach, Meshach, and Abednego. They had a hot time but didn't get singed. King Neb, ever observant, noticed there was a fourth man in the furnace with the teens. The king was amazed and gave honor to God and promoted the three. A big payoff for their commitment.

Few of us will ever have to risk our lives to save a whole race of people like Esther did. We'll probably never face a fiery furnace because we won't renounce our beliefs. But we might risk popularity or "coolness" by standing up for a kid who's being picked on at school. We could risk being part of an "in" group by refusing to participate in the things others might do that compromise our values. And we might risk giving up some of our free time to dedicate ourselves to serving others, raising money to free slaves, and educating people around us to the plight of the voiceless and powerless.

Another Look at Standing Firm

Rosa Parks

Almost everyone knows who Rosa Parks is. She has become famous for her act of defiance in refusing to give up her seat on a bus to a white person. But I think it's hard for some of us today to really understand how courageous her actions were.

BE THE CHANGE

Even though Rosa Parks was living in a fairly modern society, that society was segregated. Segregation is when there are laws that say people of different races do not all have the same privileges. The segregation laws in some parts of the United States during the 1950s kept races separate from each other in many public places. The very idea of segregation is, to me, almost impossible to fathom. I just don't get how in a civilized world something like that could have been going on. With that in mind, let's get back to Rosa Parks' story.

December 1, 1955, started out like any normal day for Rosa Parks. She woke up, got ready for work, and left her house for the bus stop. Each day she was forced to pay at the front of the bus then exit and walk up the stairs in the back. I can just imagine her frustration in having to experience that humiliation day after day. Then after a long day of work (she was a secretary for the NAACP), she again would pay at the front and have to go up the back stairs like a second-class citizen.

Well, on this particular day, she got on the bus after work and sat down. At the next stop, several white people got on. The bus driver glanced back and told Rosa and the people around her to move. The other African Americans around her stood up and shuffled to the back of the bus. But Rosa stayed seated. The bus driver told her if she didn't get up he'd have to have her arrested, to which she replied, "Then you may do that."

Rosa refused to give in to this injustice. Some people have

suggested she was so weary she couldn't stand up, but that was not the case. It wasn't that she was tired physically; she was just tired of surrendering. When she sat down, she was really standing up for an oppressed people. Her people. She could have just stood up and moved so a white person could have her seat, but she didn't.

Rosa's refusal to give up her seat was one of the turning points in the history of civil rights in the United States. Her one act of quiet, peaceful defiance triggered a series of protests and boycotts, including the Montgomery Bus Boycott, in which almost all of the black people (and some whites) in Rosa's hometown of Montgomery, Alabama, refused to ride city buses for more than a year. They were tired of segregation, and they refused to put up with it any longer.

I'm afraid there aren't enough people like that today; people willing to stand up for their own rights and the rights of others. Rosa Parks remains an inspiration to those who have the same dream. The dream that one day all of us will not only be able to live together and tolerate one another, but that we will love and stand up for one another as Jesus loved us on the cross.

In her autobiography, Rosa talks about how she hated being the center of attention. But that didn't stop her from continuing to fight for equality by any means. She participated in the famous march Martin Luther King led from Selma to Montgomery. At one point during this march, she was actually put out of the

march by someone who didn't know her. You see, the march-
ers had to wear a special color of jacket in order to participate
in the final leg of the march. Rosa was not informed about this
and was kicked out several times, only to be pulled back in by
someone who knew her.

I once read that when Rosa Parks was a child, her grand-
father used to sit awake at night with a gun on his lap in order
to protect his family from the Ku Klux Klan. Surely her life was
marked by oppression and discrimination. Yet rather than being
overcome by bitterness and hatred, she chose to act for justice
for herself and others.

What about You?

Living Out Standing Firm Today

A lot of us are willing to stand up for ourselves, for our own rights
and concerns. But are we willing to stand firm on behalf of others?

When Adolf Hitler was rising to power in Germany, a
German pastor named Martin Niemöller became aware that
Jews and other racial and political groups were being persecut-
ed, arrested, and even killed because of Hitler's racist policies.
Niemöller became one of the leaders of the Confessing Church,
a group of Christians within Germany who vocally opposed
Hitler. Because of his outspoken criticism, Niemöller himself
was locked away in a concentration camp from 1937 to 1945, and

narrowly escaped execution. After he was released, he wrote the following poem about the need to stand against evil:

> First they came for the Communists,
> and I didn't speak up,
> because I wasn't a Communist.
> Then they came for the Jews,
> and I didn't speak up,
> because I wasn't a Jew.
> Then they came for the Catholics,
> and I didn't speak up,
> because I was a Protestant.
> Then they came for me,
> and by that time
> there was no one left to speak up for me.

Many students these days stand up for things. They stand up for their favorite bands, brands, and their own personal "rights." But are these things really worth your time, energy, and commitment? Is that the kind of "hill you want to die on"? I didn't think so. Is it better to stand up for someone or something that is right or to stand up for yourself? What if we put more energy toward the things that really matter instead of spending so much energy on petty things?

I can tell you what would happen. There would be a lot fewer hungry people, a lot fewer dying children, and a lot fewer slaves in the world. If we spent more time putting our heads together and less time butting them, think of what we could accomplish! We could do so much with the time we often spend on petty things.

Is there anything you're willing to stand for (or sit for, as was the case with Rosa Parks)? I hope it has something to do with contributing to the greater good and not just expanding your own territory.

This doesn't just apply to big issues like slavery; it can apply to many other day-to-day situations. If you see someone picking on the smallest guy in the grade, you stand up for him, right? If

Therefore, my dear brothers and sisters, stand firm. Let nothing move you. Always give yourselves fully to the work of the Lord, because you know that your labor in the Lord is not in vain.

1 Corinthians 15:58

someone makes a racist comment, you speak up, right? And if someone makes fun of Jesus Christ, *you don't tolerate it.*

We're under an immense pressure to conform to this world's way of doing things. If we don't go along, we might get mocked. (Oh no! Not that! Anything but that!) Plain and simple: We should stand firm for what is right, just because it is right.

The Amazing Change

Standing Firm in Action

What kind of pressures are students under just to go along with the status quo?

What would you do today if you were a white person who got on the bus where Rosa Parks was seated, and she got up to give you her seat?

Would it be easier to stand firm if you knew there was a pay-off here on earth like the promotions Shadrach, Meshach, and Abednego got?

What kind of oppression and injustice have you observed? What can you do about them?

Standing Firm

Be the Change!

Students have a lot of buying power. Find out about the issue of fair trade by searching online. Make a decision not to buy anything you suspect may be made by slave labor, and support products that are certified fair trade. Also research companies who are producing products that are better than fair trade.

Read Isaiah 1:17. Ask God to give you opportunities to use your voice to seek justice for others.

Take the title page of this chapter to the copy center (or use a home scanner if you have one), and make a reduced copy of the page small enough to fit in your wallet or purse. Keep this with you to help you stand firm when you see injustice or when you are tempted not to live up to God's standards.

PASSION

"THEY CHARGE ME WITH FANATICISM.
IF TO BE FEELINGLY ALIVE TO THE SUFFERINGS
OF MY FELLOW-CREATURES IS TO BE A FANATIC,
I AM ONE OF THE MOST INCURABLE FANATICS EVER
PERMITTED TO BE AT LARGE."

William Wilberforce (1759–1853)
British politician and abolitionist

Take a Look at Passion

William Wilberforce

William Wilberforce inspires me. He had an all-consuming passion that drove him to overcome the obstacles that came his way. Even though Wilberforce lived two hundred years ago, his passion has not died; it is carried on by people who are working today for the same cause to which he devoted his life.

William Wilberforce was elected to Parliament (Great Britain's version of our Congress) when he was only twenty-one years old. Even at this young age, he had the virtues essential in any good government leader: passion, motivation, and courage.

For most of his life, Wilberforce suffered from a serious disease. It was punctuated by sharp bursts of pain in his stomach, violent coughing, and severe pain throughout his entire body. Sometimes he refused to take his medicine because it would dull his mind. He said he had to be on his toes to do his job. You see, Wilberforce believed God had called him to abolish the slave trade. God had given him a big idea with the passion to get it done.

Wilberforce waged countless attacks on the slave trade throughout his time with the British Parliament—nearly twenty years! But he didn't do it alone. He was part of the Clapham Sect (which I discussed in the Community chapter). Wilberforce and his group were a powerful force in the movement to end slavery. They sold books, wrote songs, and made pamphlets about the abolition of the slave trade. One of the biggest things they did was collecting signatures on anti-slavery petitions that were rolled out in front of Parliament. On one of the petitions, they collected 390,000 signatures. And they did it all without the Internet or an advanced mailing system!

Even so, their efforts were not immediately successful. At one point a discouraged Wilberforce decided to go and consult with his old pastor, a former slave trader named John Newton. Years before, Newton had come to Christ while on a slave ship during a storm, but it had taken him awhile to put his faith into practice and turn away from his slave-trading ways. But eventually Newton changed his course, and wrote the familiar hymn "Amazing Grace," which describes how God had freed him from his own captivity.

When William Wilberforce showed up at John Newton's church, he was too nervous to knock on the door. In fact, he walked around the block twice before he mustered up the courage to go and talk to Newton, but I bet he was glad he did. Newton gave him words of advice and encouragement, imploring him not to give up on his cause.

Even with all the effort and support from his friends in Clapham, for many years Wilberforce was unsuccessful in his efforts to abolish the slave trade in England. But he refused to give up. Finally, in 1807, the Slave Trade Act passed by a vote of 283–16, abolishing the slave trade in the British Empire.

But William Wilberforce's life's goal was not complete. For the rest of his life he continued to fight against slavery of all kinds, working to better the culture until the day he died.

Another Look at Passion

Erik Lokkesmoe

"Basketball was my life from junior high through my senior year of high school," says Erik Lokkesmoe. "I spent five to seven hours a day practicing, running, weight training, working on tedious drills to improve foot speed, ball control, and so on. I would even fall asleep shooting the basketball in the air while lying on my bed at night. It was all I thought about. A bad game would affect my mood for days. I was on a roller-coaster ride of emotions based on my performance."

Erik Lokkesmoe picked up a basketball during junior high, and he didn't want to let go. He ate, slept, dreamt, and lived basketball for several years of his life. His goal was "to play in college, to hear the roar of the crowd, to see my name in the paper." Basketball became his only identity. "Outwardly I would say, 'It is all for God's glory!' Inside I relished the attention, the accolades, the sense of belonging and recognition."

Sometimes, when you are doing something bound to bring you recognition, it's hard not to get a big head. Like, if you're a high school freshman who plays on the varsity football or basketball team, you will definitely get recognition for that. It feels pretty cool to get attention for something you've done. It makes you feel special when kids at school high-five you in the halls and tell you you're great. Or it can be hard to be humble when adults tell you they admire you for your work on an important project.

When people learn about the work I do, they sometimes make a big deal about it. That's why I pray God will help me to be humble, so he doesn't have to do something dramatic to get my attention back on him. Literally, I've asked God, "Please help me humble myself so you don't have to do it for me." I don't want to get too full of myself, or make some big mistake that could humiliate me and ruin my reputation, credibility, and future opportunities.

The world Erik Lokkesmoe had around basketball came crashing down halfway through his senior year. His favorite coach—the one who had been grooming him to lead the team—suddenly resigned. Then a chronic injury forced Erik to sit out the rest of the year. All he had been working so hard for was taken away. In Erik's words, "It was as if God was saying, 'You have learned what you needed to learn, Erik, and now I have something else in mind for you.'"

The only other thing that came close to basketball's importance in Erik's life was art. Erik spent most of his lunch periods in the art room—building, sculpting, and creating. "I have always

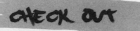

CHECK OUT

Want to see the artword of a student who's using her gifts and passion to bring beauty to the world? Then check out the amazing art on Akiane's Website at www.artakiane.com.

been fascinated by creativity, the imagination, the realm of the arts," Erik says.

After completing school, Erik moved to Washington, D.C.—a city he calls "the most *uncreative* city on the planet." He moved there thinking the only way to impact culture is to make laws, but he soon discovered this was not so. Even in D.C., there was room to make an impact through the arts. He has found out God uses the poor and downtrodden, the brooding artists and the lonely poets. Erik believes this is because "they are like soft clay, not brittle like so many who have fame and power and influence."

Erik started an organization called Brewing Culture, which brought together faith, the arts, and culture. He made a difference by helping cultivate artists and using the arts and popular culture to get people to think deeply about God.

When Erik's passion for basketball was interrupted because of an injury, Erik could have become bitter and discouraged. Instead, he pursued another, very different passion, one that would go on to impact the arts and faith community in positive ways.

What about You?

Living Out Passion Today

I am passionate about a lot of things — some more important than others. If you've read this far, you know that one of the things I'm most passionate about is the abolition of the modern-day slave trade and human rights for the oppressed. I have learned the stories of modern-day slaves and they deeply disturb me — especially when I live in a country that prizes freedom. I want to do all I can to end the sale of human beings, and I believe my generation is the one to get it done.

If ending slavery is also your passion, that's fantastic. But if it's not, I'd encourage you to find out what your passion is. Sometimes our passions can become obsessions, and this is not healthy. But when we submit our passion to God and explore it with him, we can bring help to the world he loves. In fact, in my book *Lose Your Cool* you can walk through some of the ways you can uncover your passions.

One of the things I love about Erik's story is the diversity of his passions. Most people wouldn't think a jock would be an art lover. Maybe some guys on the team would have made fun of him because of his interest in art. And he might have found it just as hard to fit in with the arts crowd. It's great that Erik didn't let stereotypes keep him from pursuing his passions. Maybe one reason he's got influence today is because he can relate to many different kinds of people.

PASSION

What are you passionate about? If God has given you a passion for something, you probably have a talent that goes along with it. The question is: What are you going to do about your passion and your talent?

Let me tell you a story: There were these three guys who were working at a tech store over the summer. They'd all been best friends for what seemed like forever, even though they were very different. One day the store manager approached the three young men to test their financial abilities. He said, "I'm going to give each of you a sum of money to invest in anything you want. In thirty days I want you to bring back the money I gave you, and however much you have made." With that, the manager gave each of them $10,000 and told them to go out and do what they had to do.

The first guy went and bought stock in a taco stand and earned twice what he was given. The second guy bought a small restaurant (okay, a *really* small restaurant — but the food was great) and ended up making just $1,000. The third guy put his money in an old gym sock, put the sock in a shoe, the shoe in a box, the box in a bag, and the bag in a safe he buried in the ground.

At the end of the thirty days, the manager called the three employees to his office. He asked the first man to give him the money he earned. Guy number one pulled out a check for $20,000 and handed it to the manager. The manager said, "Well done! You get a raise." And with that he handed the guy back the check.

Then he turned to the second guy. Almost on the verge of tears, the employee handed him the $1,000 he'd made: "I really did try to make a go of my own business. I really did try to make you proud, sir." The manager smiled and patted him on the shoulder, saying, "I understand. You made me proud, and because of that, here's $10,000." The man jumped up and ran out of the room as happy as could be.

The third guy pulled out the sock filled with cash and said, "Here's your ten thousand bucks. I buried it under the ground so I wouldn't lose it. Aren't you proud?"

But the manager's face clouded over and he said, "I gave you the money and told you to do something with it, and you, in turn, buried it under the ground. Because of this, you will not get a raise. In fact, I'm gonna split this money up and give it to the other two guys as a Christmas bonus! But here's your sock back." The third man walked away dejected and confused, without fulfilling the purpose he had been given.

If you think you've heard a story like this, you probably have — because it's very similar to one of Jesus' parables. (You can read it in Matthew 25:14-30 or Luke 19:11-27.) In this parable, God is the manager, we are the employees, and the money is our passion and our spiritual gifts. If we choose to invest our passion and gifts like one of the first two employees, God will be happy

> ## "Let me do all the good I can, to all the people I can, as often as I can, for I shall not pass this way again."

John Wesley (1703-1791)
Pastor, theologian, and abolitionist

with us, and we will have fulfilled our purpose here on earth. But if we are like the third guy, our heavenly reward will be smaller. So who do you want to be: the passionate world-changer or the apathetic couch potato? It's your choice.

If you have the gift of poetry, find a way to use your poetry for good. If you are gifted in athletics, do your best at your sport (without obsessing over your performance) and look for ways you can bless others in your sport with compliments, encouragement, and pointers that will make them feel important and more confident. Use whatever gifts God has given you for the good of others; that's why they were given to you. When we catch a vision for how God wants to use us and our gifts, the excitement, energy, and enjoyment that comes to us is the very definition of passion. And passion applied to a cause can change the world.

The Amazing Change

Passion in Action

William Wilberforce was passionate about justice and freedom—not just for himself but also for others. How do you see yourself to be like him or different from him?

What are you passionate about? You may want to explore the question with your friends, youth leaders, parents, or other people who know you well. Consider the things you really care about, the things that are often on your mind, and the things you're willing to sacrifice for.

PASSION

In what ways can you use your passions for good? Brainstorm on some ideas for marrying your passion with someone else's need.

What do you think of the idea that if God has given you a passion for something, he probably has given you some talents to use that passion for good as well?

Why might someone lose their passion for something? Does it always come back? Explain.

Passion

Be the Change!

On the back of the title page for this chapter, use all capital letters to list the things you know you're passionate about. Then write in lowercase the things you think you're passionate about or things about which you might develop a passion.

Tear out the sheet and put it inside the front of your Bible. Ask God to provide you with opportunities to use your passion for him and others.

Learn more about modern-day slavery at **www.zachhunter.me** and find out how you can continue the work of William Wilberforce.

Also, watch the film *Amazing Grace*, which is about the life of William Wilberforce. On the bonus features I walk viewers through a tour of the National Underground Railroad Freedom Center in Cincinnati, Ohio.

"Whenever I hear anyone arguing
for slavery, I feel a strong impulse
to see it tried on him personally."

Abraham Lincoln (1809 - 1865)
U.S. president and abolitionist

LOOSE CHANGE TO LOOSEN CHAINS

students freeing modern-day slaves

What's It All About?

Loose Change to Loosen Chains (LC2LC) is a student-led campaign to rescue victims of modern-day slavery. According to *Simple* magazine, $10.5 billion in loose change is lying around in U.S. households. Loose Change to Loosen Chains emphasizes three simple steps to get students involved in raising funds for this cause:

1. **Educate** Family, Friends, and Community on Modern-Day Slavery
2. **Collect** Change through Various Activities and Drives
3. **Submit** Funds and Success Stories

Through LC2LC we can join the long line of abolitionists who have fought to bring about freedom from slavery. Working together we can end slavery in our lifetime!

Modern-Day Slavery

In *Be the Change*, you've learned that millions of children, women, and men are held as slaves in the world. Sometimes they have borrowed a small amount of money to pay a debt such as a medical bill. They then find themselves in bondage to the money-lender and may work in a rock quarry breaking rocks by hand, making bricks, rolling cigarettes, cutting gemstones, or trapped in brothels. Victims are often beaten or threatened with violence if they try to leave or aren't productive enough.

Who Benefits from Your Loose Change?

There are a number of organizations actively involved in many aspects of emancipation and abolition work. You and your group can research these organizations and decide where you will invest the funds collected through Loose Change to Loosen Chains. In this section, I have included some recommendations for you. These organizations are working to:

- Prevent enslavement of vulnerable people
- Rescue victims of slavery
- Provide legal advocacy that leads to prosecution of slave holders and traffickers
- Support aftercare and restoration services for people coming out of slavery
- Educate people about the global problem so slavery can be ended

Getting Started

To get started, you can go to www.zachhunter.me and download all of the tools to launch your own abolitionists' campaign. This includes PowerPoint presentations, order forms, devotionals, stories, and lots of other cool stuff.

It's great to have you on board. Follow me on Twitter @zachjhunter and let's stay in touch.

How Students Are Using Loose Change to Loosen Chains

Student groups around the world have launched LC2LC campaigns and have tweaked it to make it work in their community. All the tools are easy to use and customize. Some student groups have added other activities around the campaign to raise more awareness and funds and involve more people. Here are a few of the ideas students have successfully used.

Dramas

Students in Georgia were putting on the production *Seussical Musical*. Playing off of the Dr. Seuss statement that "a person's a person no matter how small," the students used the production as a way to raise awareness about child slavery. LC2LC buckets were available at each performance, snacks were sold to raise money, and information was printed in the playbill about the campaign and abolition.

Community Events

Summer can be a hard time to hold student-led events, due to people dispersed in their communities. To reach the community during this season, some students have used events like summer festivals, county fairs, and street fairs as a way to raise funds and awareness. Often the community organizer will allow students to set up a table free of charge, collect loose change, and hand out information. One student group even set up a dunk tank, asking leaders in their community to be dunked to loosen chains.

Concerts

Local schools and youth groups have added concerts to the LC2LC effort including Rock for Change, Jam for Justice, Rock for Freedom, and other cleverly titled events. Ticket sales go to benefit abolition, and students use the concert as a launching-off point for the coin collection drive.

Runs

Several communities have held fun runs, 10K runs, and other fitness events to raise funds. Students in Washington State, Ohio, Virginia, and elsewhere have used these events to engage more adults in their communities.

LOOSE CHANGE TO LOOSEN CHAINS

Join the effort and launch Loose Change to Loosen Chains in your community. All the tools you need are at **www.zachhunter.me**.

Check these organizations out and determine which one you'd like to invest in through your LC2LC efforts:

- **Compassion International** ~ www.compassion.com
- **Free The Slaves** ~ www.freetheslaves.net
- **International Justice Mission** ~ www.ijm.org
- **Love 146** ~ www.love146.org
- **GoodWeave** ~ www.goodweave.org
- **Makeway Partners** ~ www.makewaypartners.org

To download the Loose Change to Loosen Chains toolkit, go to **www.zachhunter.me**.

NOTES

NOTES

Generation Change
Revised Edition

Roll Up Your Sleeves and
Change the World

Zach Hunter

Real world. Real people. Real time.
Real change.
    Inside this book you will find stories
about real people doing amazing things to change the world
around them. You will discover a new sense of wonder about
what can be and how you can help make it happen. You will
encounter voices of justice and hearts of compassion. You will
be inspired to find your own spark—fuel that will help ignite a
generation of change.

> *Our generation has seen the hurting world in living color. The
> media has brought every major human rights, health, and en-
> vironmental crises right into our living rooms.... It's easy to
> complain about what's wrong with the world today. But I think
> my generation is tired of hearing complaints and excuses, and
> we're eager to see people get busy and do something about the
> problems.*
>
> —Zach Hunter

Lose Your Cool
Revised Edition

Discovering a Passion that
Changes You and the World

Zach Hunter

You don't love a mocha the same way
that you love Jesus.

As a teen today, you probably have
plenty of interests and plenty to plug into. In the midst of the
constant stimulus—activities, media, text messages, and social
networking—activist and fellow teenager Zach Hunter asks:
What consumes the bulk of your time? How do you zero in on
what really matters?

Zach wrote this book to share powerful inspiration from
the lives of others and to promote his steadfast belief that his
generation is capable of great things—actions that may require
shedding conventional notions of what is cool and important—
and of choices that can heat up, ignite, and stoke the flames of
a deeper passion, the kind of passion that changes the world.

Are you ready to lose your cool?

Available in stores and online!

ZONDERVAN®
.com